Praise for Good Grief

Recognizing grief and despair after loss are a matter of survival. Cheryl Barrett's, **Good Grief,** *can assist us to begin a healing journey and reweave the story and social fabric of life and community that have been changed forever. Barrett's words help us touch our deepest soul's wisdom that restores and generates the hope, courage, and vision needed to find a new way of being.*
    — Barbara Dossey, PhD, RN, Author,
    Florence Nightingale: Mystic, Visionary, Healer; Holistic Nursing: A Handbook for Practice; and *Nurse Coaching: Integrative Approaches for Health and Wellbeing.*

Thank you, Cheryl, for sharing your story, your vulnerabilities, your challenges and your courage to renew in ways that all of us who have been through loss understand and feel in that deeper place of being. You connected us and made it real. The practical tips you shared to help others, I felt, create a healing pathway in very simple terms, yet we know and acknowledge that the journey of grief is far from simplistic in nature. Your words allowed tears to surface, release and your humor made me smile.
    — Anah Aikman, NZRGON, NC-BC, Nurse Coach,
    The Road Less Travelled at www.theroadlesstravelled.co.nz

Cheryl has written a book from her heart bringing together her own experience of grief and loss after the sudden death of her husband of 46 years and her years as a nurse helping others at the end of the life of their loved ones. She gives very concrete help in how to surmount the challenges of the loss of a spouse, including resources — all shared in such a comforting, loving, compassionate voice. I felt as if I was sitting with her in her living room.
    — Kit Racette, Grief Edu-Therapist, Author,
    Elizabeth where are you? A journey through grief.

D0869278

Avoiding the great loss of a loved one or dear friend escapes no one. From her own personal experience, Cheryl serves as a wonderful guide for others on the same journey. If you only adapt one or two of these strategies, you will move out of the darkness and into the light once again. Peace.

— **Brian Luke Seaward, PhD, Author,**
Stand Like Mountain, Flow Like Water and *Stressed is Desserts Spelled Backward.*

This book acts as not only a guide, but a testimony of overcoming grief. Cheryl is very real and sheds light on how grief can not only affect your emotional, but physical and social health as well. The reader can truly empathize with Cheryl's story and is provided with many useful tools on how to deal with the devastating effects of grief with a holistic approach. I highly recommend this book to anyone struggling with grief and looking for a hand to hold to get through their situation.

— **Daniel Wilson, DC, Neurologically Based Chiropractor**

Cheryl Barrett's book, **Good Grief***, is a love story. It takes the reader's hand step-by-step as one who has lost her husband, her other half, and begins to rebuild her life towards wholeness without him. It is an honest, open and sensitive exploration of her healing journey of transformation and resilience. With more than 30 years of experience as a registered nurse to draw from, she shares a variety of practical information to help others navigate the pain of such a loss and the courage to find hope and purpose. I recommend this book to anyone struggling with these issues as a resource to navigate…the journey from darkness and despair to hope, light and transformation.*

— **Catherine Errico, MSN, HWNC-BC, HN-BC, Nurse Coach**

After losing a loved one a year ago, my journey through the grieving process has been one of pain, loneliness and often despair. Cheryl's book, **Good Grief***, offers me inspiration, motivation and vision. A vision of healing and restoration. She provides guidance on restoring the mind, body and spirit while helping one to understand the uniqueness of their own journey.*

— **Glenda Bundy, RN, BS, NC-BC, Nurse Coach**

Good Grief

Strategies for Building Resilience and Supporting Transformation

David,

God bless you as you journey through the process of grief and of sharing your experiences and love of God with others.

Cheryl A Barrett
6/4/2022

Cheryl A. Barrett, RN, MSN

outskirts
press

Disclaimer

*This book is dedicated to my loving daughter, Bonnie Barrett,
who has been by my side, sharing her love, compassion,
caring and outstanding sense of humor.
And in memory of my husband,
her father, Frederick Charles Barrett, Jr.*

How to Use this Book

This book is a "must read" for those experiencing the grief and loss of a loved one. There is no easy path through grief and loss, but a path of ups and downs — a few steps forward and a few steps backward. It is intended to share what I learned to move through the process of grief and loss, with tips for how you can, too. However, with persistence, you can heal and successfully move through grief to the next chapter in your life.

This book contains stories of personal successes and failures, organized into sections identifying specific issues encountered during the grieving process. Quotes are included for each section that add depth; added as well are a few poems — some of which are mine, inspired by my own grief and loss.

There are self-help tips in each section to provide you with useful information for coping and making it through a tough day. Add a few of your own if your like. Whatever works for you is good. Worksheets provide concrete examples and a plan to stimulate you to engage in the healing process.

Affirmations are included for each section, a few words or a phrase that are positive statements that when said may help you to engage the power of positive thinking. These positive statements create a shift from the downward and inward emotions/feelings to the upward and outward emotions/feelings. For example: a shift from despair to hope by the power of words. Make a list of your own affirmations, even copying some of these, to carry with you when you are feeling…not so positive.

I have also included a list of resources for dealing with grief and loss, a sampling of what is available to assist you in coping. A few of the resources are intended for health professionals wishing to improve their skills in caring for those experiencing loss.

As with any book, you can read it from cover to cover at your own pace and then come back to a concept that resonates with you. You could also read it a section at a time and contemplate how your situation can be helped. However, I suggest you review the table of contents and choose an item that speaks to a specific need you have at the moment and use the tool, affirmation or other helpful suggestion that is included. Feel free to write in your book, underline what is important to you, or dog-ear pages to come back to.

This book was not written overnight, but over many months that became a few years. It started out as a journal, and as time went by, it turned into more. I wish that I had a resource like this to help deal with the emotions and everything else that arose during my own grieving process. Instead, I learned by trial and error.

I hope reading this book brings you a sense of shared experience during your grief, as well as bringing you some comfort. Also, I want you to realize that there is hope for a future, maybe not what you originally planned, but one that is fulfilling and joyful.

After all, you have always had your own special path to follow. A path along which wonderful people and events enter for a time and then exit — this journey is the process of LIFE.

Table of Contents

Words of Gratitude i

Foreword v

Introduction vii

A Note on Grieving xiii

Emerging from the Darkness xv

My Story 1

Comfort Each Other 9

Be Courageous: Ask for and Accept Help 17

Accept Hugs from Family, Friends, and Strangers 21

Pace Yourself in Exposing Others to the Loss 25

Condolence Check List 29

Carry Sunglasses with You at All Times 31

Keep Tissues Close by Your Side 35

Take a "Time Off" from Work 39

Fake It till You Make It 43

Make Lists of Things that Need to be Done 47

Funeral Choices 53

To Do List 55

Eat Something Every Day 57

Take Care of Yourself Physically and Mentally 61

Plan Self-Care Activities for YOU 67

Self-Care Activity Worksheet 71

Visit the SPCA or Hug Your Pet 73

Acknowledge Guilt and Regret, then Move On 79

Resource Lists: Books and Movies 85

Embrace Forgiveness 87

Recognize the Humor in Situations:Laugh Alone or with Others ... 93

Resource Lists: Books and Movies 101

Beware of Anticipatory Grief.. 103

Recognize the Signs of Depression and Take Action 107

Depression Action Plan 113

Take Time to Be in "The Present" 115

Pray Every Day or Do Whatever Feeds Your Spirit 121

Keep a Journal... 125

Adapt to Change: Losing Bits and Pieces of Your Loved One 129

Memories of Loving You 134

Moving On and Moving Through... 135

Be Prepared for a Calendar of Event Triggers 141

Revisit Places of Shared Memories... 145

Be Aware of Blessings and Express Gratitude 149

My Wish for YOU 152

Allow for Time to Heal Your Wounded Spirit............................. 153

Muscles of the Soul Worksheet 161

Witness to Others What You Have Learned on Your Journey 163

Resources 165

About the Author... 171

Review This Book 173

Words of Gratitude

Gratitude, the state of feeling grateful, is a powerful concept and one of my most used tools in moving through grief and loss. I believe that expressing gratitude releases a tangible energy, expansive in nature, with infinite potential. When I express my gratitude, I am saying that I have a grateful attitude. It is an energetic change that becomes a part of me that I share with others creating a positive impact for both of us — the giver and the receiver. It is greater than the sum of its parts. Gratitude has been like an investment — the more I gave, the more I received.

I did not think this way at first. I could see nothing to express gratitude for during my journey through grief and loss. I often had to remind myself to find things, sometimes only one thing, to be grateful for. This changed over time as I wrote about my loss and received support and caring from others. I became filled from within as I found more and more things to be grateful for, more and more opportunities to express gratitude, and more and more people who expressed gratitude to me for sharing my story of loss and recovery.

This book is written in gratitude for everyone in my life and everyone yet to come into my life, as well as both the visible and invisible forces creating the oneness of all. I am grateful to those who have been on this journey with me — both near and far. Thank you for your support, guidance, presence, witness, comfort, sharing, caring and helping me heal.

I am grateful to God for His presence in my life, for His guidance and loving support. I never questioned my faith, but asked a lot of "whys." This book was a work of love and healing inspired by faith, hope and the best of who we are as human beings.

My deepest and most sincere gratitude goes to my daughter, Bonnie Barrett, who has been by my side as she too journeyed through the grief and loss of her father. We are a team who have shared joy and sorrow, learned to forgive and to move forward confidently with strength and grace. I love you.

My humble gratitude and best wishes go to Brian Luke Seaward of Paramount Wellness for writing my foreword and supporting me through the book-writing process. He included two concepts that I could not find the right spot for in my book: reference to the stages of grief by Elizabeth Kübler-Ross and Joseph Campbell's template for The Hero's Journey. I first met Luke, in 2011, when I took his stress management instructor course. This course provided the stress management foundation which I repeatedly referred to for survival strategies on my own "Hero's Journey" through grief and loss. A giant hug to you, Luke!

A special thank you to Douglas Winslow Cooper, my editor and firm believer as a "completionist." This may not be a legitimate word, but presented a powerful challenge for me to complete my book and join the ranks of the "published." I would still be writing and editing this book if not for his attention to detail and supportive push to the finish line! And much gratitude to Outskirts Press for guiding me through the publication process.

A gracious thank you to Barbara Dossey for welcoming me on the path to integrative nurse coaching and holding space for me to be all that I was meant to be. I learned not only how to coach others, but to practice coaching myself through difficult times "to find a new way of being." She was responsive to my queries and requests for support offering solutions, kindness and wisdom of the whole.

I am grateful to Bonney Gulino-Schaub and Richard Schaub for their support and guidance as I started my journey through grief and loss while attending their classes on transpersonal coaching. Some of my grief work was done using techniques from this class.

A heart-felt thank you and big bear hug to June Amarant, my dear friend, who lost her mother shortly before my loss. She has been my heart-companion throughout the grieving process. We have learned from, and supported each other. I am grateful that she asked me to be her mentor for her MSN in education. It gave me something to focus on and get outside of myself during a time when I just wanted to withdraw from life. Congratulations to us both. We made it!

Hugs and gratitude to two people who supported me on my quest for self-care, reviewing my book and providing encouragement to completion: Dr. Daniel Wilson, my chiropractor, and Dr. John Kempter, my holistic dentist in NC.

Thank you to my colleagues, friends, and friends of friends who embraced my request to review and/or endorse my book. You provided the much-needed encouragement, validation and momentum to complete this project. Thank you, Anne Rowley from PA; Anah Aikman from New Zealand; Libby Parker from Canada; Maureen Powers from AK; Glenda Bundy from TX; Kit Racette from Canada; Margaret Schmidt from WI; and Catherine Errico from NJ.

Finally, but no less important, much gratitude to all the wonderful strangers who knowingly and unknowingly cared for me on my journey through grief and loss. You will always have a place in my heart.

Foreword

As a health psychologist with an expertise in the field of stress management, one of my mentors of the allied health profession was the renowned psychologist, Elizabeth Kübler-Ross. Known throughout the world for her work on the topic of death and dying, she not only shed light on the stages of the grieving process from loss (i.e., denial, anger, bargaining, withdrawal and acceptance), but taught several generations of people from around the world how to move through the grieving process with grace and dignity.

I learned many things from her over the many decades she served as my mentor, role model and friend. One of the most important aspects I learned about life was how to embrace the grieving process — and move through it. Too many people, she would often remind me, get stuck and don't know how to get home again. "Returning home again is a metaphor for returning to wholeness," she said.

Another one of my heroes and role models in the field of psychology and human potentials is the renowned cultural mythologist, Joseph Campbell. Although I never personally met him, I have been greatly influenced by his collective works. His template of The Hero's Journey is a sojourn that we are all on. Perhaps the greatest trial of each hero is to face their own death; to learn to grieve and move on.

Taking that first step out of the darkness and into the light is the realization that death is an illusion; yet, the emotions we experience through any death process are very real. As we evolve, the strength of the human spirit through the maturation of these emotions, moving from fear to love, we illuminate the hero's journey pathway even brighter for others, making their journeys that much more bearable.

No matter how long or short your time is here on planet Earth, you will experience loss. This is part of the human condition. With each loss, no matter how big or small, we are ultimately faced with a choice: to either wallow endlessly in the pit of despair, or to emerge from the darkness of grief, into the light. Experts will tell you that grieving is normal, grieving is healthy, and everyone grieves in their own way, all of which is true. Experts will also tell you that prolonged grieving is unhealthy. Prolonged grieving becomes a dead end, and offers no way to get back home, no way to return to wholeness.

While you may feel alone, even stuck on your journey, remember you are never alone. You have friends, both seen and unseen. If you are holding this book in your hands, then you have quickly learned that one of your new friends is Cheryl Barrett, who serves as a wonderful guide.

Cheryl's book is filled with many great tips, suggestions and guidelines to move gracefully through the grieving process and come through as a victor, not a victim. Cheryl has been there. She has experienced heart-breaking loss, and she has come through the other side gracefully. She has, in the words of Joseph Campbell, "returned home." In doing so, she offers you this book: a map and compass of sorts, to get you back home again, home to a sense of peace, home to a sense of wholeness.

Welcome home!

Brian Luke Seaward, PhD
Author, *Stand Like Mountain, Flow Like Water*
Stressed Is Desserts Spelled Backward
Paramount Wellness Institute
Boulder, CO
www.brianlukeseaward.net

Introduction

Who am I? I am you. Who are you? You are me. We are ONE —
connected through the drama of living and loving, working and
playing, caring and sharing, birth and death, grief and loss, joy
and sorrow. Yes, we are ONE — engaged in the story of life, and as
time passes, we learn to celebrate who we are and who we are be-
coming as we continue on our path — our individual journey: the
survivors, recovering and creating a new story.

— Cheryl A. Barrett, Nurse Coach, Author

We all experience loss during our time on earth: loss of a spouse, parent, child, pet, home, jobs, etc. We are born and grow to understand the impermanence of our existence with no life expectancy date. However, most of us go through life with little or no thought to our mortality, making no preparation for our departure or preparation as the survivor of a departed loved one or the loss of something significant to us such as a home, pet, or job.

The impact of any loss depends on the value, worth, or significance of a specific loss, as assigned by each person. The experience of loss is personal and impacts the mind, body, and spirit of the primary person involved, as well as a network of others: immediate family, extended family, friends, colleagues, and community.

Your loss begins with great sorrow, but there is hope as you courageously take the first step on your healing journey. I was reminded of this by the saying in one of the sympathy cards I received:

To know sorrow is to acknowledge the love
that was yours…
To carry on with a heart full of memories
is wholly and lovingly human…
To heal, day by day, is to build a bridge of love
that will reach far beyond time and into forever.
— Ambassador Cards

You may wonder what gives me the right to write about grief and loss. I do not have a psychology degree nor have I done extensive research in the field of death and dying. I have not written books, been quoted by experts or appeared on a TV show. I am an ordinary person — one who has recently lost a husband and gone through the process of mourning his death. One who has struggled with putting the shattered pieces of my heart and life back together…a survivor of grief and loss.

Besides being a grieving woman, I do have experience with death, grief, and loss. I am a nurse with over 30 years of caring for patients, families, and loved ones. I have worked as a nurse in a variety of jobs: as a bedside care nurse in the hospital on a medical/surgical unit, telemetry unit, and intensive care unit (ICU); as a professor of nursing, teaching in a college and university in the classroom and the clinical rotation sites in hospitals; as an administrative supervisor in a hospital; as an editorial director for a nursing publication; as an educator and director of education in home care, and now as a nurse coach and mentor.

Through the years of nursing at the bedside, especially in the critical care area, I have had the honor to participate in the grieving and loss process with many patients and families. I have witnessed families face the sudden, and often traumatic, loss of a loved one and not know what to do, where to begin, what is the right thing to do, whom to call and more. I have held family members as they cried and when there were no tears, gently provided the comfort of touch and caring.

I have always had an inner need to comfort others. Here are just two stories of my experience with death and caring that have touched me and helped prepare me for my own journey through grief and loss.

One story involved a patient who came into the ICU with a sudden heart attack. The prognosis was grim, at best. The son stood by the bedside, eyes gazing downward at his father, eyes filled with hope of recovery even as he was wringing his hands.

I started talking to him. He revealed that he did not get to tell his father, before he died, some things he regretted.

I brought a chair and put it by the head of the bed, next to his father's head and said, "Patients like this who can't speak and who look like they cannot comprehend anything, are often reported to still hear things."

I suggested he sit in the chair and tell his father what he wanted to say now. As I pulled the curtain and left him alone with his father, I saw him sit in the chair, lean closely to his father and start whispering in his ear.

About two days later, when I was off duty, I got a call from my unit that this patient died. I quickly got in the car, came to the hospital and sat in the waiting room with the family, including this son. The son was the last to leave. He felt lost, with nowhere to go.

So, we went across the street to the restaurant and sat and talked for a little while. He told me he was glad to have had the chance to tell his father what he had on his mind. We parted, and he went home. I was a stranger allowed to participate in the personal grief of another and to witness his suffering...not knowing then that I would also have strangers participate in my own grief and suffering.

Another story is of a patient who was dying after a long illness. As an ICU nurse, I have developed intuition, a kind of "knowing" when a patient's condition worsens. I thought, *he's not going to make it through the night.*

Indeed, that was the case with this gentleman. His wife was at the bedside, and he was connected to many wires and medication lines. I could see from the monitor how the heart rate was changing, losing stability and slowing — its bleeps farther and farther apart. It just happened to be about the time that the wife usually went home.

Understanding what I saw happening with the patient, I asked her, "Would you like to be with your husband when he passes on?"

She said, "Yes."

So, I told her I was not sure, but this is what I saw and maybe she should stay. He passed away not long after that. His wife was by his side in the lounge chair I brought in for her, with the patient's side rail down, and she was holding his hand, stroking it gently.

The next step was to call the son, which I did.

When I asked his wife if she would like to stay with me while I performed some final care for him…and participate herself, she said, "Yes."

Postmortem care is not for everyone. But, I was led to ask her. As we washed her husband and put a clean gown on him, she gazed lovingly at him and stroked his brow. She told me the story of her husband: what a good father he was, how she loved his beautiful blue eyes and more. On several occasions during our time together, I left the room to go cry, overwhelmed with emotion. One day in the future, I would do this gentle care for my own husband upon his death, and use the image of this experience to draw strength.

Nothing in my training and experience prepared me for when it was my turn to face a significant death and go through the grieving process. I went to school for nursing for six years — a challenging pursuit culminating with a graduate degree and have taught nursing students in the academic setting. I am an Integrative Nurse Coach and Transpersonal Coach officially recognized by the American Holistic Nurses Association (AHNA). I am also board-certified by the American Holistic Nurses Credentialing Corporation (AHNCC) as a Nurse Coach. I learned theory and process about grief and loss during these years and have, of course, participated in the lives of those who have crossed my path in health care situations.

None of the textbook stuff really helped. Oh, I remembered the Stages of the Grieving Process and what the coping strategies were, but that was not what I needed.

What I needed I could not verbalize. I was a strong person. I could handle this. I did not want to expose my vulnerability — my neediness. That's not who I was. But who I was…was about to change drastically. I was no longer a wife, partner, friend, lover, and more. I became a widow and progressed along a journey into the unknown…as you will read in this book.

I'll share with you my personal story of loss and the stress management and self-care strategies that I identified along the way through the healing process, strategies that can be personalized and applied to any loss.

We are unique individuals with unique needs and talents to implement self-care healing practices. We grieve and we love… in our own individual way. The journey through this healing process is not measured in time, but in each heartbeat and in each breath.

A Note on Grieving

Grieving shifts the spirit into darkness,
Pulling it right and pushing it left,
Turning it upside-down and inside-out,
Twisting it into knots and coiling it tightly with fear
Until it's difficult to breathe or move.

In the darkness of this shift,
The spirit weeps a river of tears,
The heart shatters into pieces,
And the soul screams in agony,
Exposing the rawness and pain of loss.

Time passes as the spirit undergoes a rending and purification —
A shedding of old ways and old thoughts,
A redefining of priorities and of letting go.
Each layer shed creates new soil for the soul,
A soil in which new seeds are planted in the darkness.

Seeds of possibilities destined to bear fruit,
Germinating in the new fertile soil,
Seeds readied through the struggle and strife,
Overcome by prayer and belief, laying the soul bare,
Opened, aware — waiting in anticipation.

These seeds: Hope, Gratitude, Compassion, Empathy, Love, and
Forgiveness,
Sprout forth into the spirit and grow strong,
Nourishing the soul,
Healing the pain and heartache,
Welcomed with open arms — hesitant yet needy.

Reaching for the light and hope for a new beginning,
As the shift into the light brings transformation.
Moving out of the darkness, turmoil, and strife,
The spirit is reborn, a heart is healed,
And a beautiful soul emerges.

Cheryl A. Barrett
2/23/16

Emerging from the Darkness
— Cheryl A. Barrett, Artist, 2017

This acrylic painting was created by me after I joined the Mooresville Arts Gallery, Mooresville, NC, in 2017. The inspiration came from a photo of an art object set in concrete outside the art museum in Hilo, Hawaii; however, it looks nothing like the original.

My painting took on a life of its own as inspiration welled up from deep within me, demanding a black-and-white representation of hope and despair both vying for attention. As I watched the picture take form, I felt I was living my poem. Now my poem had expression through art, and writing, both easing the pain of loss.

I have emerged from the darkness, transformed by this soul-wrenching experience of grief and loss: — to become healed and move forward on my own journey through life.

My Story

On September 1, 2014, at 12:25 a.m., I lost my husband, friend, and partner of 46 years. He was also a great dad to our daughter for 45 of those years. He was 69 years old and had enjoyed many years of retirement while I continued working. During this time, our roles shifted, and he took over the household tasks: doing the dishes, clothes washing, bed making, banking, and was the financial manager and cheerleader for me and my daughter.

My husband passed away in bed as he slept right next to me. The only thing that woke me was the snoring for which I turned and shoved at his shoulder — annoyed that I was losing sleep. I got no response and immediately became alarmed. I leapt from my side of the bed to run to the other side, to shake him and try to rouse him…with no success.

My daughter ran from her bedroom and started CPR while I called 911.

We are both nurses, so we did our routine CPR activity (pushing on his chest to help his heart beat and breathing into his mouth to bring air to his lungs), but this time with a more personal impact.

The emergency medical team (EMTs) arrived quickly, but it seemed to take forever. Time goes slowly during critical events such as this. I remember running down the stairs and out the door to flag down the team; the numbering of our town homes does not follow a logical order to enable it to be easily found. They took over the job of trying to save Fred's life, but he did not respond to their efforts.

They could not get air into Fred's lungs nor a breathing tube inserted to use as an airway, all bad signs. I requested a pause in CPR at one point to check his heart monitor (for heart rhythm) and breathing — there was no response. No heartbeat, no breathing — my husband was gone.

My daughter and I looked deep into each other's eyes and nodded in agreement, deciding to honor my husband's wishes of no heroic treatment in cases like this, as he had stated many times in the past. A hard decision to make when we could see him lying there.

We knew he was already gone, but we still wanted him back with every part of our being. When we shared our decision to stop CPR with the EMT leader, she contacted the hospital MD, and the lifesaving efforts ceased.

The coroner was also contacted, routine for deaths at home. We were lucky we did not have an obstacle with the coroner to deal with… my husband was under the care of a physician, and his medical history was evident.

When I was asked about which funeral home I would be using, I could not think of an answer. I criticized myself for not knowing the name of the funeral home our family used. *I should know this,* I told myself.

Then I remembered its location. The EMT leader knew the name and the phone number. She contacted the funeral home for us and gave us the time they would arrive to pick up the body. We said our goodbyes and thanked them for all their care.

The hardest part of this was to wait in the stillness after they all left — just the three of us: wife, daughter and the body of our loved one lying in the bed upstairs.

We went upstairs to talk to him and say our last goodbyes, to touch, to grieve together and to cry. I kissed his forehead and stroked his face, knowing that this would be the last kiss and last touch.

I was crushed. This event was unexpected — a total shock. We had survived past stressful events with him, when he had strokes and seizures, but he always recovered. This time was different, he was gone from us forever. We were in shock and felt numb. The loss of Fred's body, spirit, and energetic presence was so profound.

As I've mentioned, I am a nurse and worked in critical care at one time in my career for 12 1/2 years; I have been at the bedside when death came quietly, sometimes not so quietly, to claim a patient — another person's loved one. I have assisted family members doing postmortem care at the bedside after a death.

I have cared for critically ill adults and even "predicted" that they would die on my shift. Although I kept this to myself, it enabled me to suggest that the family member should stay a while longer. I have allowed the family to be present during the "code" of their family member, but only if this was their wish. I have supported nursing students through the patient's dying experience, including postmortem care.

Even after all this, I was not prepared when death took my husband. I was still faced with the same questions that I helped so many others to find answers to when they faced the loss of their loved one: What to do first? Whom to contact? What about work? How is Bonnie, my daughter, taking this?

So many decisions to make…it was overwhelming. The only thing I could do was one thing at a time: one breath, one step — and then another.

The first week, we did all the things that needed to be done immediately: contact family and close friends, sharing the loss as well as the plan to honor his wishes.

First and foremost, we wanted to honor his wishes to be cremated and have his ashes distributed at Daytona Beach, Florida. So, we made the arrangements with the funeral home for cremation, death certificates, payment, etc. Fred also wanted no viewing or memorial.

After this, we packed up and drove from Pennsylvania to Florida. My daughter drove the whole way down and back. We spent some time in silence. We also rehashed the details of his death, trying to understand what happened, whether we missed something, or if we could have done something more. We reminisced about the good times and the memories. We cried sometimes and used up many tissues. Other times, we shared smiles and laughter.

It took two days to arrive in Florida. When we rode into Daytona Beach, the first sight we saw was a rainbow over the ocean. We spotted this as it was developing, and we pulled the car into a parking lot to take a few photos. It seemed a sign of hope and confirmation that we were doing what we were supposed to do, bringing him to the place he loved.

We've been to Daytona on vacation for many years, and it felt like coming home. This time we stayed in a motel we had never stayed in before. We weren't ready to revisit our usual accommodations.

We spent two days thinking about what to do next and visited some of the favorite eating/drinking places he loved. When we shared our loss with one of the waitresses at a place we frequented, she hugged us both, with tears in her eyes. We felt comforted. She shared the impending loss of her grandmother; she was glad to talk to someone who knew about loss…a shared experience.

Finally, we decided to have our ritual ceremony at the beach near the lighthouse he loved to climb. He could no longer make the climb the last couple of years due to his health. We did this last act of love for him with a celebration on the beach — just the two of us. My daughter created a sand angel next to the heart we traced in the sand with his name, the dates of birth and death, flowers from his mother and sister, and his favorite sandals. A cloud in the distance out in the ocean had visible rain pouring down — as though the universe cried with us, sharing our pain. We have a photo of this, including the sand display; we felt Fred's spirit come to rest in the place he loved so much.

As we stood side-by-side, knee-deep in water, we spilled his ashes into the Atlantic Ocean, surprised at what happened.

"They are sinking," I said. "I thought they were supposed to float."

No one tells you that these ashes are different than the typical ashes from a fireplace. These ashes were the bone fragments of what remained of Fred — a weight of over 9 pounds.

Another way we paid tribute to my husband was to visit his favorite place in Daytona Beach — the Ponce De Leon Inlet Lighthouse. We arranged for a memorial brick to be placed on this historic site's walkway in his memory. (Weeks later, we received a small remembrance brick to keep with us.)

As we did this, we remembered our last trip to Daytona as a threesome, just a little over three months before his death. The first week he spent with Bonnie and her friend, who left at the end of the week. I followed, a week later, to join Bonnie and Fred. We had a great time as usual. Bonnie and I didn't think we'd return so soon and under such sad circumstances. After a week away from home, taking care of this sad business, we returned to our new reality: two, rather than three of us. The next week we spent comforting each other, doing routine chores and lots of paperwork resulting from the loss of a spouse.

Looking back, I remember well our last day as husband and wife. We spent the day together doing errands, then visited the reservoir near us to check the water level. We have water stock, and this was something he kept track of, as well as the share price. I wasn't feeling very well and did not go out to dinner when he asked me to, so he visited his favorite off-track betting site, watched a few horse races, and had a bite to eat. Things progressed as usual at home. I never thought these would be our last moments together.

I was glad that our whole last week together was filled with wonderful memories like this. He ate all the special foods he liked (courtesy of his daughter), and he went to the places he loved to go. Still, we wish we could have had more time, did things differently, said things more lovingly, been better, etc....

The door closed on this chapter of my life, joined together with my husband. Another door opened, forcing me to step through alone, cautiously and reluctantly into the unknown, not knowing what to expect, nor how to survive.

So, I tried to re-establish a life of normalcy in a life suddenly, drastically changed through the loss of a life force that had accompanied me throughout most of my life. I felt this loss of Fred keenly at first, but I tried hard to "put on a good front," "to fake it till I made it."

Fortunately, I was supported by friends, colleagues, and even strangers I met who somehow had heard the news of the loss. They sent cards, called by phone, made personal visits. These were frequent at first, but soon tapered off. I did not live alone nor need to pick up the pieces of a broken life by myself. I was lucky that my daughter lived with me, and we had a shared experience to bind us as we moved forward.

I was also fortunate that I had a deeper strength that I could draw from — my faith. Some call this a belief in God, while others may call this source of strength by another name.

To sustain this normalcy, I continued working from September, when Fred died, until I retired in January. This time was fraught with anxiety, fear, conflict, love, comfort and caring — to name only a few emotions. As time went by, I was progressively left to my own devices, often adrift, wondering what to do.

My daughter had planned a vacation to Hawaii in January with a friend and decided for me to come along, so I would not be left alone at home. I struggled on this vacation, feeling guilty about going, yet happy for the opportunity. I kept wondering how my husband would have enjoyed this or that. Guilt followed me everywhere, as the learning and growing process continued.

My daughter and I have gone on many learning trips in the past and are already nurse coaches. I love learning. My daughter and I signed up for a course on Transpersonal Coaching in New York for April — only seven months after our loss.

While there, we practiced awareness exercises, just as we had in other courses, but this time it was different. One exercise we did was to be guided to seek our wisdom figure to answer a question we had. I had trouble deciding on my question, so I started the experience with just an open mind and heart.

As I got to the part of the experience where I was to meet my wisdom figure, I saw a blurred figure moving toward me, with no specific shape at first. I saw the form changing, becoming white and slender. I kept watching. More details evolved, yet not so many that a face was recognizable.

When the figure was close enough to touch, I felt extreme longing. I reached out with both arms and turned my head to the left to lay it on the chest of the figure — an action I've done frequently in the past when hugging my husband. My hands seemed to bump into white, wing-like structures that enfolded me. As I embraced the figure, he embraced me.

The figure spoke to me, "It's going to be OK."

I had been wanting a hug from my husband, and I had gotten it. I fought accepting this at first, then let go of my unworthiness and was grateful it had happened.

The healing continues but is not over.

It's been over three years since the loss of my husband — but it feels like only yesterday at times. In one sense, time froze that fateful day; and yet, time still passed, 24 hours in each day ticking away as usual. Days moved into weeks, then into months, and now years.

I had no control over time. Neither will you — even if you try. I continue to take a few steps forward and then slip a few steps backward in my healing journey. Sometimes, I get stuck for a while. Other times, I make much progress and growth. The growth phase has been scary. I often wanted to stay in the past, more comfortable, and less daunting than moving forward. But, forward I moved each minute, each hour, each day, continually.

I asked, "Why?"

I wanted one more day. I was angry, sad, confused, lost and lonely. As time passed, the sorrow eased. Then came the holidays, special events, and other things that exposed my feelings of grief and loss again. I keenly felt the heartache and relived the pain, only to work through the healing…yet again and again.

You see, I went through the grieving process in my own unique way, as you will, too. Guess what? I learned a lot. I am grateful for my daughter's invaluable love and caring. Bonnie is a beautiful, empathetic young woman who is also going through this journey of grief and loss in her own special way.

You and I, we are not alone. I am not different from anyone else in having to experience sorrow. I have a story of loss. Everyone eventually does.

In this book, I have shared some of the experiences that helped me heal on my journey through grief and loss. I hope you find comfort in the stories and use some of tips I discovered to help you when you are stuck on your healing journey and find it hard to move forward.

Comfort Each Other

If there is any kindness I can show, or any good thing I can do to any fellow being, let me do it now, and not deter or neglect it, as I shall not pass this way again.

— William Penn

Take a moment to ask yourself this question: What does "to comfort" mean to you?

It may be simple to come up with an answer or it may be a challenge. You may come up with different terms to describe comfort than would your friend, relative, or colleague at work.

Whatever description you have for what comfort means to you is valid; it will reflect what your comfort needs are during times of stress. Write them down somewhere you will have easy access to them when stressful events knock at your door, because you may be overwhelmed and likely to forget them during such times.

If you know what comforts you, then when someone asks you, "What can I do for you?" you will be able to tell them what you need to get you through a tough time.

Comfort for me meant that someone would care enough to take the time to share with me their caring, love, and support. I did not have a list made ahead of time, but I had a good understanding of how to give comfort…as any good nurse does. What I did not have was the experience of being a receiver of comfort and caring — so I had to learn how to receive.

I found that there were some specific things that comfort meant to me:

- the companionship and love of my daughter and her wonderful cooking — reminding me of our connection;
- someone dropping everything and coming to my home to give me a hug and hold my hand while listening intently to my story of loss with tears in their eyes — making me feel worthy of love and caring;
- others sharing their memories of my husband with me — reminding me he will be forever in my heart;
- someone calling me on the phone to talk to me and continuing to keep talking when I could not speak — filling the empty silence;
- someone to stuff tissues into my hands when I cried and could not see to find them — allowing me to grieve and them to witness;
- being wrapped in a big loving hug and held — for more than a few seconds, making me feel grounded, connected, and safe;
- someone willing to let me decide how to spend our time together — making me feel special;
- enjoying laughter with my daughter (the comedian) or a friend — easing the pent-up tension;
- someone allowing me to sit side-by-side with them in silence, holding space for me and my grief — creating a protective space to just be;
- receiving such lovely condolence cards from everyone — each one unique, offering a special message just for me; and
- me "giving" comfort and caring to those who were also comforting and caring to me — recognizing their hurt and feelings too.

Below, I have shared some acts of comfort and caring that met my needs and provided me with outstanding memories.

At first, I was wrapped up in my own world of shock and grief. The environment around me was a blur of activity or a void of nothingness. I wanted to shrink into myself or lash out at others for no apparent reason. But then I recognized that I was not the only one experiencing the loss and grieving. Everyone was feeling the pain and loss in their own way: my family, the EMT group who tried so diligently to revive my loved one, the undertaker and his assistant, as well as a host of others. I found myself reaching out and comforting others as I witnessed their grief response — often suppressing my own. This may be a natural response for some; yet, others may retreat into isolation for a while as the pain and shock of the loss is too overwhelming.

There is no wrong choice for dealing with this loss — it is a unique experience for each individual and for each loss. I can, however, say that reaching out to comfort each other is a very powerful action. It has a twofold healing benefit, as the grief and loss are shared experiences: not only for the person experiencing the immediate loss, but for those sharing in the loss of someone they cared about. Sometimes, we can only stand beside one another and let our closeness say what words cannot. Other times, we can accept invitations out for coffee and a chat or lunch, dinner, or just a walk. Having someone to talk to and grieve along with supports the wounded spirit and eases the loneliness.

My first act of providing comfort and receiving comfort was from the EMTs during the resuscitation event. We talked to each other as professionals, as I am also a nurse with a background in intensive care and am familiar with these types of events in the hospital setting. The team leader was sensitive to my needs when I said that my husband's wishes were not to continue heroic measures in a case like this, lacking success in the resuscitation process.

We stopped the process, ended it officially. They gently put my husband back in bed. I thanked the leader and the team for their caring and respect. The team leader stayed and helped with a phone call to the undertaker for me. I knew which one I wanted, but could only remember the location, not the name. This being taken care of, the EMTs left.

My daughter and I sat alone together on the sofa in the living room side-by-side, staring, as the aftershocks of disbelief, pain, and grief enveloped us…our minds were still reliving the event.

I could not sit still. I went upstairs to the bedroom where my husband remained. My daughter's first act of comfort to me was when she followed me up the stairs and stood by my side while I touched my husband and kissed him good-bye. She and I needed to be close. We had just lost a very significance presence — my husband/her father. Being physically close, whether exchanging words or sharing the same space in silence, is comforting.

My first comforting act for my daughter was to sleep in the same room with her after my deceased husband was taken to the funeral home. He had died in my (our) bed. I could not sleep there. Bonnie and I had a hard time sleeping, so we just lay in bed and tried to rest until morning came…with its myriad of duties awaiting us.

My daughter and I went to the funeral home together and took care of all the arrangements — feeling a sense of honoring him by following through with his wishes. By caring for him in this way, we were caring for ourselves, as well.

We also discussed finances and the routine home upkeep duties/ obligations that do not disappear during this time. I needed to remember to take my time, ask for help, and move forward to the next task. My daughter and I looked after each other, despite forgetfulness (especially me) with leaving doors unlocked, forgetting paperwork, lights left on, etc. We sent each other text messages via phone while we were at work to keep connected.

Later in the grieving process, I wrote a note to my daughter telling her that I was proud of her, loved her, and that she was awesome. I taped the note on the wall in the bathroom where she would find it. When she did, she came and gave me a big hug. She left that note hanging in the bathroom for weeks.

Sometime after this, my daughter went away for a few days. I was home alone for the first time. She left me quite a surprise — a total of nine, yellow, Buddha post-it notes were scattered around the house. I found them on mirrors, in my books, on my computer, on the TV, in a picture frame, etc. Each note contained a special caring comment: "I Love You," "You are Awesome," "Breathe," and others. It took a while to find them all. Each made me smile and shed a few tears. I also felt joy for the first time and so cared for by my daughter. This act validated that the caring had come full circle — back to me.

One day, I was taken out by a friend, Kathy, who asked me what I wanted to do: "Do you want to be quiet, talk, walk, sit on a bench? I'm here for you whatever you want to do."

She let me decide how and what experience we would share together. *It was all about me.* I could decide how to receive comfort that I needed — or what felt right. I had trouble thinking of what I wanted to do, so I decided to go somewhere close and familiar. We stopped by a park with a pond and a small waterfall. We sat on a bench side-by-side and just listened to the sounds of nature while we said a few words to each other. I was blessed by her presence and this gift of companionship.

Others provided comfort and caring to me in their own unique ways. I appreciated each person's willingness to step forward and offer me such precious gifts.

My achievements included answering the phone, responding to email, texts, or knocks at my door. These were challenging for me, resisting the tendency to withdraw into myself and build a wall of protection — insulating me from having to talk about the loss. Although withdrawing sounds like a great idea at first, do not prolong this protective phase. It is important to connect with people, to talk about your loss, to receive caring from others.

Note that I do not normally "just answer the phone," so this was significant for me. I decided to pick up the phone and accept the comfort of friends and family. Phone conversations were strained at first, with pauses at times when either the caller or I struggled for what to say. I remember a phone call or two in the beginning when I got so choked up and could hardly talk, and the person on the other end could hardly understand me.

If I had made the call, I feared the person would think me a crank caller, as I tried to speak around the sobs and said to them, "Don't hang up. It's me and...."

Then the news of my husband's death came out between sobs. Slowly, I gained control and spoke.

I also answered the door when friends came to the home to participate in grieving with me and my daughter. One friend, Kathy, called and came over with flowers and sat with me for a while, providing comfort and companionship.

Another friend, Annmarie, called and said, "Cheryl, just give me your address, I'm coming right over."

And she just showed up on my doorstep without delay, greeting me with a bear hug and much compassion. We sat on the sofa and she leaned in toward me, fully present, as she listened to my tale of woe.

I would like to offer a few words of caution here, as some comfort givers have little experience in this area and either avoid you or stumble blindly in their attempt at caring. Some people have been culturally conditioned in their responses and may seem robotic in their offerings of care. And many, frankly do not know how to provide caring, because tragedy and loss have not crashed into their own journey through life — yet.

My suggestion: listen to all who offer you caring and support, however it comes, with an open heart. Hold your criticism at bay. Judge not how the message is delivered, but hold dear all who dare to care. This is an opportunity for all to learn about the messy business of grief and loss. We know that 100% of us will deal with death at some point. There is no escape. It is up to us how we deal with it — and we each deal with it uniquely.

I learned that comforting and caring for each other has no set of guidelines to follow. It is important to listen to your heart and respond when you sense someone's pain, suffering, grief, or loss. Remember to be gentle with yourself when reaching out to comfort another. Be genuine, be yourself, and just be there for them and yourself too. There is no right or wrong way to care. Just choose to care.

AFFIRMATIONS:
- I am worthy of love and am loved.
- I am grateful for the caring of others.
- I feel comfort by sharing my grief with others who care.

Be Courageous:
Ask for and Accept Help

*Ordinary men hate solitude. But the Master makes use of it,
embracing his loneliness, realizing he is
one with the whole universe.*

— **Lao Tzu,** *Tao Te Ching*

Few people are mind readers, so don't expect them to know what you
are feeling or what you need!

This next concept is important to grief processing — at least in my
opinion. **"Ask for help!"**

I repeat, "Ask for help!"

Just do it. Here's why: Asking for help can decrease both your
stress and the helper's stress significantly. Don't be surprised who you'll
find placed in your path of need. Set your intention to positive! Expect
that there is someone waiting for you to ASK. "If you build it, they will
come" has as its corollary, "if you invite comforting, it will take place."

This was a hard lesson for me to learn. I had many conversations
with myself about whether I should ask for help or not. Of course, I
asked God in my prayers — but that was easier than exposing my vulnerability by asking people I knew.

I was about to learn that I could ask and I could receive and still feel OK.

I felt so alone with the loss of my husband; we had lived side-by-side in each other's presence for so long. When I was out and saw other couples, twosomes like my husband and I used to be, I felt even more lonely and withdrew into solitude. I was ONE, no longer part of a couple. Indeed, in some sense, I was a HALF of the person I had been for so long, now disconnected from my other half.

It took time to come to terms with the martyrdom of keeping it all together and to "tough it out" by myself. I was drowning in arrogance and self-pity. I needed to dig my way out. The key was to acknowledge my inability to "do it all," and instead accept the help others wanted to give and even — to ask for help! This was hard. I have been a self-sufficient woman for many years. My change in attitude to needing, asking for and accepting help had some amazing results.

Guess what? Some friends don't know what to do, what you need, or how to offer help — a real eye-opener. So, what did I do? I started asking for help, and was rewarded by smiles and sighs of relief from my friends. My loss was really "not all about me" but included so many others, as we are all connected with the universe. We are told not to ask for whom the mournful church bell tolls…it tolls for each of us.

Some memories of how I asked for and received help from both friends and strangers are included below.

I was out for a drive and called my friend, Anne, at her home and said, "I'll be driving by your house on my way from work. Could I stop in for a hug?"

"Ok," she said, "but don't mind my messy home."

I did not care what the home looked like! I was focused on the physical comfort of a hug and the comfort I would feel being with my friend. I did stop by, did not notice any messiness, and got more than her hug. Her husband, Jim, hugged me, too. I also received licks from the dog, nudges from the cat, and kind words from her son. There is something to be said for the benefits of pets. They seem to know when a person is hurting and they just stay close. I felt so cared for sitting at their table, surrounded by friends and pets and sipping a cup of tea.

Two days after my husband died, I went to Target to get some romance novels (my usual coping/escape mechanism when under stress). When I came out, the car wouldn't start. At first, I sat there in shock, not believing this was happening.

Looking up to the sky (and thinking Fred was watching), I said, "Are you kidding me?"

This was followed by a few choice words I'll not mention here. I could just picture and hear him having a good belly laugh.

Then, I went into problem-solver mode and checked the dials on the control panel, the gas gauge, and anything I could think of that could be causing the problem. The electric windows worked. The lights worked. So, why didn't the car start? There were too many signal lights on the dashboard to identify an easy solution — I was a woman, after all…some would say.

I looked around the parking lot, thinking someone would appear and know that I needed help. Not so easy, because when alone, you are fearful of reaching out for help from a stranger. It was now dark and starting to rain, with strong gusts of wind. I was afraid to ask the person in the white car parked beside me or the person in the black truck in front of me. I was alone, insecure, vulnerable, and downright scared.

So, I called my daughter, and she came to help — whew! My brave Bonnie traveled during a severe thunder-and-lightning storm to help her mama. When she tried to start the car, it did not start either — *it's not just me,* I mused.

We could not figure out the problem. We had a few laughs during this, saying, "I bet dad's just laughing so hard there are tears in his eyes."

So, we went to Plan B: We traveled in her car to the Home Depot in another section of the shopping center. I entered the store with this thought in my mind: *I'm looking for a man who knows something about cars. I need a man.*

Holy cow, that sounded creepy! Worse, finding one was easier said than done. I walked past the first man I saw behind the customer service counter, dismissed him, and approached three other employees, asking them for assistance or at least some knowledge that would be useful — no luck here.

Then, on the way out of the store, I stopped the first man I had passed and asked about the oil I had in my hand — after all, one of the lights identified low oil and seemed worth a try to fix the problem. I told him the problem with the car and that my husband had just died this week and I did not know what to do about the car.

"I am so sorry for your loss," he said. "Just give me a minute."

Then he picked up the phone and asked someone to cover for him while he went into the parking lot to help a customer for a few minutes. He came to my car, jump-started it using my daughter's car in the stormy, rainy night. Then he hurried off, even though we offered him a ride back to the store. His name was Bob, and I thanked him. A week later, I saw him again at Home Depot and thanked him again for his care and help.

I learned that asking for help was not such a hard thing to do and that exposing my vulnerability allowed the experience of asking and accepting help from others to happen. I even found out that those who responded to my request for help felt good about having the opportunity to be of service. Everyone needs to be needed in some way, and everyone needs to help someone in some way.

> *Ask, and it shall be given you; seek, and ye shall find; knock, and it shall be opened unto you.*
>
> — **Matthew 7:7**

AFFIRMATIONS:
- I accept myself and acknowledge my needs.
- I make my own choices and reach out to meet my needs.
- I am courageous and fearless, knowing others await my requests for the opportunity to care for me.

Accept Hugs from
Family, Friends, and Strangers

He tells me I look as if I could use a hug and I laugh at him and he
ignores me and steps forward and puts his arms around me and
hugs me. I warm at the simple pleasure of human contact and for
the first time in a long time I actually feel good.

— **James Frey,** *A Million Little Pieces*

What is touch? I am talking about the kind of touch that is an exchange between you and someone else. When you are young, you touch and are touched frequently through the routine contact of parenting, playing, sports, friendships, etc. You get pats on the back, hugs, handshakes, you wrestle with siblings and more.

Surely you can think of times you have enjoyed the touch of others or wanted to reach out and touch someone to offer comfort. Touch is so important. Scientists have found that if an infant is deprived of touch, this can lead to developmental delays as well as growth and cognitive impairment.

Research indicates that as we age, touch occurs less frequently and that adults and elders deprived of touch feel disconnected, isolated, lonely, and often depressed. This may be due to living alone, hospitalization, illness, isolation or other causes.

Touching practices also vary according to cultural mores — some groups being very much touch-oriented and others more distant. Take this into consideration when you are offering hugs to others so as not to offend. You can always ask for permission to hug.

Hugs are touches that signify caring and can involve partial or full body contact. It usually depends on the relationship. A hug feels good to the person being hugged. I remember how good it felt to be hugged (embraced in a caring manner) by someone who was trying to comfort me during my time of grief and loss. I felt less alone, and my spirit lightened as the grief was shared through this contact. I felt a sigh move up through my body followed by muscle relaxation.

There are moments in life when you miss someone so much that you just want to pick them from your dreams and hug them for real.

— Heart Centered Rebalancing

Yes, I still remember how a hug from my husband felt. I miss this dearly, but still get lots of hugs from others. I have a few hug stories that I will share with you.

I was in an orthopedic office to get a shot in my right shoulder and bicep tendon due to joint pain. When I went to check out with the receptionist, I started crying. Crying is a spontaneous thing and can be triggered without notice.

She asked me, "Are you OK? Do you need a hug?"

I was unprepared to respond, but she seemed to know what was needed. So, she did not wait for a response, but just came right around the barrier between us and gave me a big hug. She told me that her husband died at 42, and she knew what I was going through. I took a seat in the waiting room to regain my composure. Then the male physician assistant came into the waiting room and told me I could stay in the waiting room as long as I needed and he would wait to leave — no hurry.

They were done for the day, but my needs were important to them. These were both total strangers.

I started to wonder if anyone ever got addicted to hugs and caring. I added "hugs" to my self-care plan.

A little more than a year after my husband's death, I was on a spiritual retreat in Sedona, AZ, a place my husband and I had been to years before, when we traveled across the country over the span of a month. I was very sensitive to our previous togetherness adventure and at the retreat became tense, agitated, easily upset. At one event, I felt so overcome that my face scrunched up and I burst into tears. I was embarrassed, turning quickly away from the group, thankful that they were already leaving our gathering to go outside.

One person, Mariane, saw what was happening to me. Before I knew it, she was across the room, and she wrapped me in a hug from my head to my toes. For an instant, I felt uncomfortable with this hug from a stranger, but then I found myself feeling her healing energy surround and penetrate every part of my being.

The sensation was so relaxing and peaceful. She murmured comforting words and stroked my head and my back as I told her why I was crying and how hard it still was for me without Fred. The hug lasted only a few minutes, but it felt much longer. I found out that Mariane was a healer; she had also lost her husband too, so she knew what grieving meant. We were strangers sharing a common bond of loss. Both related well to the need for comfort.

Sometimes all you can do is hug a friend tightly and wish that their pain could be transferred by touch to your own emotional hard drive.

— Richelle E. Goodrich

Some believe hugs are a means of transferring energy to another person who is dear to you. When this occurs, it will replenish depleted energy at any time, particularly when a person is in need. Hugging provides the feeling of caring and compassion; it is more personal than words. It calms the mind, body, and spirit, making you feel that you are connected and not alone. My daughter and I hugged each other often. I received hugs from friends. I also received hugs from some strangers in public places. (Hugs from strangers may be perceived as threatening and stressful for some, so this may or may not be for you.)

Hugging is considered beneficial and may significantly improve your wellbeing. Some say that you need at least four hugs a day as the (RDA) **R**ecommended **D**aily **A**mount for your health and well-being. Don't forget to hug someone to show your caring. Do not forget to ask for a hug when you need one. **Give a HUG today** to someone you love…or someone who needs a hug!

AFFIRMATIONS:

- I am surrounded by relationships that feel good.
- I am worthy of love and acceptance.
- I trust the universe to provide for my needs for comfort and caring.

Pace Yourself in Exposing Others to the Loss

*One of the greatest gifts you can give anybody
is the gift of your honest self.*

— Fred Rogers, TV Show: *Mr. Rogers's Neighborhood*

One self-care survival tactic essential for me was being honest with myself regarding my needs. At this very stressful time for me and my daughter, I did not want to keep repeating to others, "I called to let you know that my husband died."

What worked best for me was for my daughter and me to make the contacts closest to us by ourselves first and to have the help of family, friends and colleagues to address other contacts.

This not only helped decrease our stress, but allowed others to feel good about being able to help and support us through this time. The night my husband died, my daughter felt the need to call my sister-in-law at his mother's home to tell her about it, so she could convey the news to his mom — a high priority. Others would be notified later. The next morning, some select others needed to be called by phone: some co-workers and a few close friends/relatives.

Notices also went out via group email to others at work, partially handled by my contact in Human Resources who offered to do this for me. I greatly appreciated this offer of support and thanked him.

The second week, individual calls were made to those who were considered close, but whom I did not see often.

The third week, I stopped at some of the businesses we were connected to and shared the loss. I also sent out emails to work colleagues or responded to the emails and condolence cards sent by mail.

Since I belonged to a group of nurse coaches, I sent an email to the leader, Barbara Dossey, sharing my loss and asked her to forward it to all our colleagues. Without delay, the message was sent and I was getting more messages of caring and support. It's so helpful to have support persons who can help you disseminate such sensitive information. I could not have imagined interacting with so many on a one-to-one basis.

Five weeks later, I continued to communicate our loss to others not yet aware of it.

Even nine months later, I was still sharing the news of Fred's demise with some in my community who had not learned of it.

There are some people you do not know how to contact, but over time they check in, either by email, phone, or snail mail. An alumni group from my husband's high school was one of these. I opened his mail, and the letter inside announced a reunion of those turning 70; it included an email contact, to whom I conveyed the news of my husband's death, asking it to be passed on to those in the group. The contact person responded with condolences and agreed. I even got a few responses from others in this group whom we both knew.

I do not know if this was the right way to proceed or not. I had no training in how the process worked, so I just pushed my way through what I thought best. You may know another, better way to share the news of a loss or have experience with rules related to the grieving process that you follow. Use whatever works for you.

Many of you also include the traditional obituary announcement that informs a larger audience of the loss of your loved one. This includes the information needed to participate in the funeral, memorial service, and gathering afterwards. Some funeral homes today also offer a posting of the event on their website with all the important information needed by those who wish to participate in the viewing or burial. These traditional communications were not pursued in our case, nor was a memorial service announcement, as it was not my late husband's wish.

The most important thing I found was to connect with those who were willing to jump in and help me through this task. I am very grateful for each one of them. To keep track of my follow-up communication to those who offered condolences, I made a list (see the next page) and used it to not miss anyone.

AFFIRMATIONS:
- I take my time in dealing with difficult situations.
- I face each day with hope and strength to move through the grieving process.
- I am gentle with myself and others.

Condolence Check List

To keep track of my follow-up communication to those who offered condolences, I made a list so I would not miss anyone. Remember this is a stressful time, and you are distracted. Use this helpful tool. You can also ask family or friends to help you.

NAME	COMMUNICATION FROM YOU: Card, Phone, Email, Etc.	DONE

Carry Sunglasses with You at All Times

The soul would have no rainbows
if the eyes had no tears.

— Native American Proverb

Grief and loss produce emotions, and tears, that emerge spontaneously — anytime or anywhere. Sometimes you are prepared for the tears. Sometimes you are not. Crying makes one's face puffy and blotchy, turns the whites of eyes red, causes the area around eyes to swell and nose to run. It's not a pretty picture at all.

I'd better stay inside, I said to myself many times. *I look scary.*

This look takes time to fade, and you may not want to go anywhere. So, instead of daring to go out and risk others seeing your grieving look, you may just stay in by yourself. Unfortunately, this condition could last for months, and you really need to meet the demands of daily living. **Step forward and break out the sunglasses!**

Alas, you often cannot find your sunglasses. Usually they are on your head, and you are too stressed out to remember — no problem. Have a couple of pairs in strategic places, a pair in your pocketbook, a pair in the car, and a pair (or two) on your head.

Ha, believe me the double-glasses-on-head look has happened more than once to me. Frantically searching for my sunglasses, I'd walk by a mirror and look up to see not one, but two, pairs on my head.

Remember, forgetfulness is part of the stress response you are experiencing, and this *preparedness* covers all bases. You may be laughing as you read this now, but note that in this state, you are not a pretty sight. You may even want to add a bit of makeup to look more presentable. However, makeup plus tears can get a bit messy. So, choose wisely.

I found that having sunglasses at the ready was an important self-care tool, helping to shield my red, puffy eyes from others. Beware, this grieving look is like a beacon, alerting others to avoid you or to venture forth attempting to comfort you. Either of these choices may lead to even more tears. You are trying to keep your emotions in control and appear normal most of the time. Sunglasses help you to maintain this control.

Unfortunately, sunglasses primarily cover the eyes; the rest of your face may be giving clues to others of your distress. You have done the best you could. Keep your chin up and venture forth to do your chores. You may even run into someone who shows you a random act of kindness during this time. It happened to me.

I wasn't sure if I was hungry or not, but I told myself I had to eat something. I did not know what to do with myself. I wanted to go out and get some food, but where? I rode to Chick-fil-A and went inside. I stood rooted to the floor just a short distance inside the doorway with my sunglasses on; as I looked around, I experienced a momentary feeling of being lost, not knowing what I was doing there or what I wanted. It was a scary feeling for me, as I am always so in control.

I was caught off guard when a stranger, an older woman, approached me, started talking to me, and handed me something. I had a hard time paying attention, but I thanked her for whatever it was she handed me. As she walked away, I looked down at what she placed in my hand — a $10 gift card for food at Chick-fil-A. When I looked up, I could not find her. As I proceeded to the counter, I tucked this gift card into my pocket and used my own money to buy my dinner. I asked myself, *why did she give it to me? I'm not needy; did I look needy? Good grief, I must really look bad!*

When I sat down and tried to eat, I was fighting back tears while thinking of her kindness, telling myself that I did not deserve this gift. There are so many others who could use this gift. I asked myself again, *what did she see in me that caused her to give this gift to me?* Then I remembered all the times I had given gifts such as these to others and went on my way, never considering how they felt. Now I wondered how they felt, and if they had asked themselves the same questions I did.

Then a thought popped into my head: *Cheryl, you are not in control, and the universe knows how you hurt and is sending people your way to provide kindness and compassion through many ways — including gifts from strangers.* So, I changed my perspective from feeling undeserving to embracing gratitude.

I was still glad I had my sunglasses as protection. **Love your sunglasses and keep them close.** You will need them often.

AFFIRMATIONS:
- I am brave and able to move forward one step at a time.
- I share my grief with humbleness and grace.
- I am gentle with myself and accept grieving as a part of life's transition to new life.

Keep Tissues Close by Your Side

Don't be ashamed to weep; 'tis right to grieve. Tears are only water, and flowers, trees, and fruit cannot grow without water. But there must be sunlight also. A wounded heart will heal in time, and when it does, the memory and love of our lost ones is sealed inside to comfort us.

— **Brian Jacques,** *Taggerung*

This will come as no surprise to you, but crying can occur at any time. You do not want to be without this necessity — **tissues!**

Often, the person you are with does not have any tissues to accommodate you and you are left with tears flowing unfettered down your face, disrupting your makeup, perhaps combined with yucky stuff running from your nose. Neither of these are very pleasant to see or feel, and you do not want to feel any worse than you already do. Let the tears flow, but keep your supply of tissues handy. You already feel bad and do not look your best. No need to add cosmetic insult to emotional injury.

"Be prepared" is my motto! Keep a supply of tissues in your pocketbook, tote bag, pocket, and car. Sometimes, I did not have tissues, and what I did was use the napkins I keep in the side door pockets of my car or purse.

If you are caught with all your tissues used up, don't be afraid to ask for them. You'd be surprised how many places have tissue boxes somewhere close by, ready to meet your needs. Often, while out shopping, I have had people that I interacted with take one look at my face and notice when my eyes got glassy (on the verge of tears again) and offer up their box of tissues, sitting behind the sales counter, before I even asked. God bless these intuitive beings!

There will be times, however, when there are no tissues available. Exceptional circumstances require breaking a few rules. So, it's OK to use your shirttail or your sleeve to do what you need to do to tidy yourself up. Remember, we used our shirttails and sleeves to do this when we were children and having that memory and skill comes to the rescue now. Don't worry, it will wash right out. No one needs to know, as you sneak a wipe here or there. You can turn it into a funny story and have a laugh with a friend. But, remember to get tissues at the next stop or keep an extra stash available in strategic locations as backup.

I found crying to be a great way to release the pent-up emotions I was feeling. I cried when I was angry, sad, frustrated, felt sorry for myself, or just about anything since the loss of my husband. Crying made me feel good sometimes, pathetic at other times. I was very hard on myself, thinking *I should be able to get a grip and buck up* — and you may feel this way too.

Be brave. Let the tears come, for whatever reason, and feel the emotional release. Use your handy tissues to mop up your tears and runny nose. Then, take a deep breath in and out or even two or three or more breaths in and out, to calm yourself. At times, all you can do at first is to breathe. Remember that you are still a part of the living. Teary episodes will become less frequent and less intense over time, but I do not think they ever go away. They haven't yet for me.

During the journey through grief and loss, you will find that your friends and loved ones have boxes of tissues ready for your use when you visit. If you run out of yours, they will give you the box to take with you. I just love my friends. When they visit me, they scan the environment looking for the tissue box so they can provide it and show caring. Tissues are not just for you, however, as those grieving with you also cry, have runny noses and need these supplies.

Remember to **share your tissues** — crying can be contagious. It is a precious gift to cry together with someone who cares.

AFFIRMATIONS:
- I accept my weaknesses at this time and allow others to share their strength.
- I am strong and I will survive one day at a time.
- I am at peace with what is happening in my life.

Take a "Time Off" from Work

Time is an illusion.
The more you are focused on time — past and future —
the more you miss the now.
The eternal present is the space within which
your whole life unfolds, the one factor that remains constant.
There was never a time when your life was not now,
nor will there ever be.

— **Eckhart Tolle**

Taking time off from work is very helpful in allowing for a recovery period, as well as allowing you time for organizing and doing all the tasks that arise related to the passing of your loved one. It also gives those at work who care about you time to collect themselves to interact with you when you return.

My suggestion to help you avoid the pressure to buck up and perform at your previous level, is to take an extended leave of absence and allow yourself time to heal. You can use family leave, saved-up vacation, or sick time. Just meet with the human resource department to work out the details. Your physician can even support you by filling out Family Leave forms. This is ideal to do, but if money is tight, you might not have the option and must return to work as usual.

Time off from work is not for everybody. Some of you, however, may also feel the need to re-establish the normalcy of a routine and thus return to work as soon as possible. Choose wisely the course that is best for you. If you come back too soon, however, and you do not progress back to the normal performance required for your job, you may be called in and criticized about this. Don't let this additional stressor happen to you. You will find out that your critics may tell you that you should have stayed out longer, anyway. So, be kind to yourself.

If you must go back to work, so be it. You will need to be strong, but also let others know how they can support you. How can they support you? Here are some suggestions, and I am sure you can think of more:

- bring you a cup of coffee or tea
- have an extra box of tissues ready when yours is used up
- go for a walk outside with you
- share a joke or funny story
- give you a hug
- give you a hand with your job

Also know that when you do come back to work, you may be comforting your colleagues as much and sometimes more than they are comforting you. You will find that you are welcomed by all and receive condolences and caring responses as the word gets out that you are back to work.

However, there is a time limit on some of these well-wisher's frequency of support, as they have other priorities and life stressors too. Oh, a few, rare colleagues will continue to care and support you, knowing full well how difficult a transition you are going through — these will be your close friends or most friendly colleagues. Some will display caring for a while, then drift off into their own world of work routine, not being malicious, but just moving on with their work — they care, but have not been in your inner circle at work, and that's OK. A few will look exclusively at the bottom line, finance and productivity, placing more stringent limits on your recovery needs. They make exceptions to your distractions, crying, and some callouts, but eventually draw a hard line. This is a fact of life in the business world.

I thought of staying out of work longer than three weeks, but decided to go back. I told myself that I had so much to do at work. After all, I am a workaholic and have been for many years. I even had the paperwork for extended leave at my doctor's office to be filled out, but I ended up not using them.

I told myself that I was strong and needed to live up to what my husband always said, "Cheryl, you are a tough old bird."

Back to work I went. In one way, it was good returning to work and having something to get up for every morning to do…even though I cried on the way to work…and on the way home from work, for many weeks. At work, I had more control over the crying — most of the time. I was always tired. I did not sleep well. I refused to take any sleeping pills. I believed that "this, too, will pass."

I appreciated all the caring and comforting gestures very much by my friends and co-workers. The hugs felt great. The sympathetic looks and kind words helped a lot. I was amazed to find out how many of these people had their own story of grief and loss of which I was unaware. This sense of a community of caring experience comforted me.

After four months, I was completely worn out with the stress of work and all the tasks that needed to be taken care of due to the loss of my spouse: mountains of paperwork and trying to keep track of the phone calls, faxes, and letters reflecting progress or problems related to the transition to my sole ownership. I decided to retire and move on — a very good decision.

Experiencing a significant loss, you are going through a very difficult time. Most people can only "imagine" what it must be like. Carefully assess your needs regarding return or delayed return to work. Do ask for help, and above all — **be kind to yourself.** You are trying so hard to keep it all together, while grieving, managing the multitude of tasks related to the loss, holding the family together, lacking sleep, having poor concentration, and crying frequently. You may really need to take a "Time Off."

AFFIRMATIONS:

- I honor my need for time to heal my mind, body, and spirit.
- I make good choices to meet my needs.
- I choose the contents of my life and am gentle with myself.

Fake It till You Make It

You gain strength, courage, and confidence by every experience by which you really stop to look fear in the face. You are able to say to yourself, 'I lived through this horror. I can take the next thing that comes along.'

— Eleanor Roosevelt

You have likely heard this expression before: "Fake it till you make it." It advises what to do when you are experiencing something that you are not very familiar with and not sure how or what is the right thing to say or do. This places you in a vulnerable position that could expose your insecurities, your lack of knowledge or skill. In most cases, your reaction is to go forward and just do the best you can — "fake it till you make it." Repetition improves your success and builds self-confidence. As your self-confidence improves, you become less vulnerable. Eventually, you do make it.

So, what does this have to do with grief and loss? The loss of a loved one creates a vulnerable period in your life. You are unsure of what to do. You are distracted and distressed. Often, depression is knocking on your door — if not already inside. Yet, your survival instinct kicks in, and you cling to the routines familiar to you, all the while dealing with difficult situations for which there may be no instructions. So, you fake it till you make it. This may be a trial and error process and may last for what seems like forever. Have faith and keep moving forward.

Some may ask: "How can I do this?"

I'll share some examples of how I did this. When I returned to work three weeks after my loss, I was distracted and bombarded with sympathy from many caring, compassionate colleagues. I felt vulnerable, lost, and raw.

Sometimes, their concern came at a good time, and I dealt well with it. Other times, their concern came at a time when I was feeling particularly sad and wanted to run away or burst out in tears — neither of which I wanted to show to others. So, I would put on a good face, take a few deep breaths, smile and continue what I was doing. I did not want to hurt those who were sharing their caring and compassion with me. This was a precious gift to receive from them.

On a good note, this did improve over time, and I became more comfortable with the process and could interact genuinely with those who cared.

Another example is when people asked me, "How are you doing?"

At first, I wanted to yell back, "How do you think I'm doing? I just lost my husband. I feel like someone just ripped out my heart! How would you feel?"

Yes, I was at war with my own thoughts. I desperately needed compassion and caring; yet, I was tempted to lash out because I felt lost and vulnerable. I knew that if I continued to lash out at others, they would flee from me in droves — the opposite of what I needed.

So, I suppressed my feelings and choose to put on a good face and give a standard reply, "I'm doing OK."

This doesn't tell them much, but satisfies their question and provides relief to the one offering the caring that they have done their duty. Whew! I "faked it" by sharing only some of my feelings because I knew they cared, while I tried to protect them from the real horror of the loss I was going through. As this war was going on, I employed the "fake it till you make it" attitude. I knew it would get easier as time passed, when my feelings eased and I started to heal.

I cannot tell you how long it will take to heal or how often you will be faking it till you make it. I am thankful for this coping method to rely on for short-term survival. However, it is not one to use indefinitely.

You must do the things you think you cannot do.

— **Eleanor Roosevelt**

If you feel unable to cope with your situation, you would benefit from help from a trained professional. You need to process your feelings, deal with the vulnerability resulting from grief and loss, and allow healing to occur. When people ask me, "How are you doing?" Now, I just say that I am sad sometimes and at other times I can be a part of the living, which becomes easier every day.

And sometimes I still cry in response. It's all OK.

However, even a year later, I was surprised that I reverted to the "fake it till you make it" technique when my friend and nurse colleague, June, asked me how I was doing. I skirted the issue and limited my talk to physical issues, but not what she really wanted to know: how was I feeling emotionally as related to my loss? I think my friend knew what was happening and was kind enough to let me off the hook. My interaction with June was the stimulus for writing this section of my book. My answer to her demonstrated to me that I was still faking it at times. This caused me to spend some time reflecting on how I really was doing in this healing process and to take the time to deal with whatever issues were surfacing.

For me, a one-year anniversary caused this protective strategy to resurface. I know it is only another bump in the road on the journey through grief and loss. And this too shall pass....

AFFIRMATIONS:

- I am strong and powerful and confident that each day brings new hope and healing.
- I trust my own inner wisdom and walk forward one step at a time on a new path.
- I know that sharing my pain will help to heal the wounds and provide others the opportunity to care for me.

Make Lists of Things that Need to be Done

*Only put off until tomorrow
what you are willing to die having left undone.*

— Pablo Picasso

Such a simple thing to do, make lists, but a huge task at a time such as this.

However, making lists of things that need to be done gives you a purpose and keeps you focused. You may have difficulty with this at first, so rely on a friend or relative to help you until you get over the initial shock. Some people find that having something concrete to do keeps them busy, giving them some respite from the feelings of loss they are experiencing.

Some people plan their transition to death prior to the event, while others come meet it with no plans. My suggestion is to at least know the wishes of each other and the name of the funeral home you want to use, as well as their telephone number.

I had been to several funerals in the past, but not as many as some. I never paid attention to the details. I just came, paid my respects, gave comfort, and left, not realizing all the details that were involved.

Fred's death awakened me to the multitude of things to be done and choices to be made. Since my husband wanted to be cremated and have no viewing or other formal celebration, our details were less complicated, less expensive, and quickly taken care of. For others, it is more complicated and expensive and lists are needed to keep track of all the details. One suggestion: discuss and plan your funeral wishes and details beforehand.

After the funeral details are completed, you move forward to the many other details that never seem to end. Financial accounts, insurance policies, joint ownership, death certificates, living expenses, debts, and many unforeseen issues arise that will need your attention. I dealt with all of this by making list...after list...after list...to keep it all together.

Keeping a notebook with divided sections really helped. Each note identifying accounts, dates, times, phone numbers, and conversations — then tracking follow-ups, next steps and completions. Tedious work indeed! I was even complimented by my financial planner, Jason, at how organized I was.

Well, if I didn't do it, how would it get done? I thought. I had no magic wand or genie in a bottle to grant my wishes.

However, I did not feel so well organized. I suggest that you have a list of all your financial accounts, insurance policies, deeds, owner's certificates, and other valuables to save you time and the stress of searching for them and not knowing what resources you have.

Funeral directors and their business managers can help greatly. Christian, at Joseph A. Ward Funeral Home in Linwood, PA, had been familiar with some of my husband's family members' funerals, but we had never really met. However, he did remember the family name, which provided some connection and comfort. I could not have asked for a more wonderful young man to assist me in this manner.

He knew the questions I needed answers to before I asked them. The check-off list he had was so helpful and offered a variety of options for the management of funeral arrangements. He also made sure I had the right number of death certificates and who needed originals versus copies. He also said he would check with my husband's previous employer, as he knew from experience that there had been insurance policies by the company for retirees. This was something I did not know. I put it on my check list to follow-up on, too. He also contacted me when there were any new developments. I am grateful for his care and compassion.

Today's funeral homes have websites that provide lists of services offered. One site I recently visited had a list of recently deceased persons with photographs. Upon clicking the photograph, you are provided with a variety of data related to this person that may include an obituary, date, time and site of the viewing and funeral, a slide presentation of memorabilia and more. Additionally, there was information on topics related to the grieving process, written by a psychologist.

Later, check lists can become a habit and lead your path for each day. The check lists may well start by including daily "normal" tasks as well. Simple tasks that you might forget if you live alone: take out the trash, pay the bills, put the recycle bag out on the specific day, go to the grocery store and others. I did this because I was forgetful due to the stress. I needed the reminders. Also, I did this because it was quite natural for me as a "detail-oriented" person.

Almost a year later, I no longer wrote as many lists that concerned the loss event. I completed many tasks through this journey of grief and loss that emerged and needed attention. It took many months to start checking off some things. You never know when something new will arise, but within a year you have had the practice and are prepared.

Keep the notebook with the lists of what has happened, especially with financial transactions. They will come in handy when it is Tax Day and you need to recall whether you rolled over an IRA or retirement money or took the cash. It can be your proof and avoid another headache. One extremely important item that has caused me much grief was dealing with utility companies. Save yourself a huge headache by closing out utility bills listed in your husband's name as soon as you can to avoid an exhausting merry-go-round ride.

Think about developing your own list for dealing with bills and finances connected with the death of a spouse:

- what are my bills?
- what banks do I have accounts in?
- what stock accounts or IRAs or 401k accounts do I have (or did my spouse have)?
- who is the beneficiary on the accounts?
- what accounts need to have a name change?
- whose names are the car and house titles in?
- what are the monthly payments if you do not own?
- are there any insurance policies on the deceased?
- who needs to be contacted?
- what should I do with funeral arrangements?
- how many death certificates do I need?
- was my spouse a veteran?
- does my spouse's last employer have any outstanding policies related to him/her?
- what are my monthly bills?
- what are my real-estate taxes, school taxes, township taxes, car insurance, homeowners' insurance, quarterly tax payments, life insurance payments, health insurance payments?
- are the payments electronic or paper?
- are payments automatically deducted from your account?
- what are my debts?

— just to name a few items that need your attention.

I know that this can seem overwhelming, so I have included two sample worksheets at the end of this section to give you a starting point. One is a sample **To Do List** and one is for **Funeral Choices**. These are not all-inclusive; you may have different information to add.

> *Don't put off until tomorrow what you can do today.*
>
> — **Benjamin Franklin**

The **To Do List** contains names and telephone numbers of all the companies I pay bills to as well as what time of the month the bill comes. I can look at this anytime to find the contact information I need. I keep this document on my desktop computer for easy access. I could also print it out if needed. Yours may contain different information. It's a great tool.

The **Funeral Choices** document contains some, not all, of the information relating to choices you need to consider when arranging for your loved one's funeral. I created this after the fact as I stumbled through the grieving process. Please know that the funeral home will have a more comprehensive list, along with individual cost for services.

I also created a finances worksheet, which is not included, in order for me to understand what my finances for the year were going to be, with just one small retirement income and Social Security. I created a spreadsheet with a column of months down the left side and a list of expenses and income items across the top. Each column would add up for a yearly total. Each row would add across to the end of the expenses or the end of the income. There was a total for all expenses and incomes. This could also be done with a paper ledger. Either method will work.

Remember to enter the numbers monthly and to check the figures every six months and at the end of the year, then make any corrections needed — I did find a few errors and corrected them as I went along. These interventions worked great for me. However, it is up to you to determine what meets your individual needs. You may even be lucky enough to know and have the help of someone knowledgeable to assist you with this, whether they be a family member, a friend or professional.

AFFIRMATIONS:
- I have everything I need for an abundant life.
- I have clarity in knowing what tasks need to be accomplished.
- I feel confident that I can meet the challenges presented to me at this time.

Funeral Choices

Keep in mind that these are very personal choices, some of which may have been preplanned, while others are determined on an emergent basis. It is important to have a knowledgeable family or friend go with you when you meet with the funeral director. I have listed some of the choices you will be faced with during this time. The funeral parlor I used had a nice check-off list that made it clear what services were available.

<u>**Topics**</u>	<u>**Options**</u>		
Choice of funeral home	Family history of use	Recommended by others	Unknown
Type of funeral	Traditional with coffin and cemetery burial	Cremation with urn or scatter ashes	Home funeral; Other
Type of service	Traditional viewing	Private viewing	Memorial
Clergy involvement	Church service	Gravesite service	Memorial service
Burial container	Coffin style and cost	Urn style and cost	Other
Burial site	Local cemetery: ground or mausoleum	Military cemetery	Urn; body donated to science; other
Flowers (often donated afterward)	Funeral parlor	Cemetery	None; donation to charity in lieu of flowers
Obituary	What to include	Cost	How to share
Sign-in book	On podium	On table	Who keeps

Funeral Choices (continued)

Topics	Options		
Prayer cards	Choice	Number of cards	Where to display
Speaker tributes	Family	Friends	Work associates
Music or singing	Who will sing	Who picks music	What kind of music
Photo tribute or video	Choice	Who to create	Who to remove
Communication regarding events	Who's in charge	Who needs to know	Method to disseminate information
Post-event gathering	Who coordinates	Where to occur	Catered or closed dishes brought by others
Other costs	Number of attendants from funeral parlor	Accessories used by funeral parlor	Hidden costs

To Do List

This can be started before a loss and helps to get things organized. OR, it can be done after the loss. Whichever you choose, you will find it a big help. Personalize your own list.

Type of Expense: Company	Frequency of payment	Whose name it's in	Account number	Phone number of company	Other
Verizon:	Monthly	John Doe			
Mortgage: Comnet	Monthly - auto debit from checking acct.	John and Mary Doe			
Aqua Water Bill	Monthly	John and Mary Doe			
Homeowners Assn.	Monthly - auto debit checking				
Master Card	Monthly	Each has			
Visa Card	Monthly	Each has			
Township Taxes	Yearly (begin of year)				
County Taxes	Yearly (begin of year)				
School TX	Yearly (July)				
Head Tax (individual)	Yearly (begin of year)				

To Do List (continued)

Type of Expense: Company	Frequency of payment	Whose name it's in	Account number	Phone number of company	Other
Car Insurance	Bi-yearly (April/Oct.)				
Health Insurance	Monthly	Each has			
Quarterly taxes	Quarterly if needed	One or both			

Eat Something Every Day

Eat healthily, sleep well, breathe deeply, move harmoniously.

— Jean-Pierre Barral, DO. and Author

The appetite is almost non-existent during this time — hunger is not felt. Food has lost its taste and sometimes it's hard to get it down.

Your friends and loved ones are telling you that you must eat something to keep up your strength, or they are just bringing food to your door until there is no place left for storage. Food is necessary for the body to function, for you to think, for you to move, for you to walk forward on the road to recovery!

I know from experience that food was the last thing on my mind at a time like this. When my husband had his stroke, I lost ten pounds in two weeks, as I worked a full-time job and tried to be at the hospital with him as much as possible. Some people might not consider a stroke to be a loss. But those who know about strokes know that a person is never really the same person they were before. You feel that loss. There may occur a small difference in speech, facial droop, memory, coordination or significant differences impacting all areas of the stroke victim's life.

When my husband was in the hospital, I got up early every morning and went to the hospital to check on him and assist with morning care, went to work, went home, went back to hospital to check on him, and then went home to TRY to sleep. As you can see, there is no mention of when I stopped to eat. Of course, I ate something, but if you asked what, I could not tell you.

The loss of a loved one, my husband, was even more devastating and could have had a very serious effect on me physiologically if my daughter had not lived with me. She was the one who made sure we both ate something every day!

I recommend just starting with small portions to eat and do it slowly, as crying can cause you to breathe incorrectly and inhale food making you cough and choke — it happens.

Also, it is helpful to try to eat with another person. It's hard to eat alone, and you will just let the opportunity pass by. Why? Because you are not interested in eating, food is tasteless, it is hard to swallow, and you just want to curl up and hide. This is easy to do when you are alone — because no one is watching. Who will tell on you?

Please remember, food is your friend on your healing journey. Food nourishes the mind and body to provide the nutrients for survival. It supplies the energy to meet your day-to-day needs.

My daughter cooked meals, so we would both eat. And believe me when I say this, she is a great cook, and I love her food! Also, have foods around that you like…they will be more appealing and easier to get down.

Another thing that helps is to make time to go out to eat together with a friend at a favorite restaurant. This provides a change of scenery, gets you out of the house, and into an environment that may distract you from your grief for a while. It also provides companionship — a comfort you desperately need. However, there were favorite restaurants that my daughter and I avoided…we were not ready to experience the emotional pain of being there without my husband yet. Slowly, we began to revisit some of the local restaurants that had memories attached to them as we became able to handle the emotions.

There may also be those who deal with stress by indulging in food

— eating to ease the emotional pain. This behavior can be just as destructive to the physical body as not eating. Overeating leads to weight gain, yet another stressor to add to your list. If you deal with your loss with overeating, you will one day look at yourself in the mirror and wonder what happened when the larger you appears in the mirror. Your self-esteem takes a hit and you can become depressed.

Either eating too much or too little has an impact on the mind, body, and spirit. My advice is to make the effort to take care of yourself, often severely neglected during times of stress. Ask a friend or family member for help to plan and support your efforts to follow through.

AFFIRMATIONS:
- I enjoy being in my body, and I nourish it each day.
- I honor my body with nutritious foods for my health and wellbeing.
- Today, I welcome health and happiness.

Take Care of Yourself Physically and Mentally

Rest and self-care are so important. When you take time to replenish your spirit, it allows you to serve others from the overflow. You cannot serve from an empty vessel.

— Eleanor Brownn, Author

Some people increase physical and/or mental activity during such times to distract them from the reality and pain of this situation. Keeping busy occupies their mind and their time and provides a self-protective mechanism used for coping. Others decrease their activity and become more sedentary and withdrawn and retreat into isolation. Either choice is an extreme with its own negative effects. Balance is the key to survival here.

Although you may have the tendency to deal with your grief and loss by withdrawing from the world, shutting yourself in darkness and curling up in bed trying desperately to block out everything, life still moves forward — you are still among the living. This, "doing nothing," is a paralysis of mind, body, and spirit that is unhealthy and of no service to you or the loved ones who care about you. Embracing this numbness and paralysis is emergency self-care at first and acts as a self-protective mechanism of survival. But remember, this is only the beginning and there is much to do and learn on your journey through grief and loss.

So, what you need to do…what I forced myself to do…was to keep moving and doing the routine tasks of living. These included cleaning the bathroom, doing the laundry, sweeping the floor, reading a book, taking a walk and other activities.

It does not matter what activity you choose — **just move!** Activity helps you get outside yourself and focus on a task, and is very helpful to use pent-up emotional energy. Doing this may even help you sleep better, too.

Others may deal with grief and loss by being constantly busy as their way to block out everything — not allowing time to really think, feel, or process the loss. Here again, life still moves forward. And although you are actively moving among the living, you are really "not living." This, too, causes a halt to the processing of life events and is of no service to you or those who care about you. So, what you need to do is to slow down and allow time to think and feel. Keeping a friend at hand or at least a phone call away for support is extremely helpful.

I continued working for several months after my husband died. Was it helpful? Yes, at first. The continued routine helped to push some of the grieving to the back of my mind. However, as time moved on, I realized that I was going in circles and getting nowhere. I was stuck in moments of grief that kept me repeating "woe is me." I was exhausting myself mentally, physically, and spiritually trying to function in both worlds: my work routine world and my grief and loss world — neither of which was going well. I had to do something before I fell apart.

Taking care of yourself is the most powerful way to begin to take care of others.

— **Bryant Mc Gill,** *Simple Reminders: Inspiration for Living Your Best Life*

So, I took a deep breath and stepped back to decide how to find a balance between too-busy and too-idle. I did this by making healthy choices in self-care for myself. You can do this too.

First, I just made simple choices. Making a big plan required too much thought and work. I knew that I needed to include both activity and rest in my physical and mental self-care plan.

I had such tension and pain in my neck and back that these created structural issues. So, I scheduled a visit to the chiropractor before we went to Florida. What a relief I got from my first visit and adjustment! Then I had another adjustment after I returned from our trip to Daytona Beach and ritual spreading of ashes in the ocean.

I asked myself, "Why did I deny myself this treatment, knowing full well that I would feel great afterward. Was I trying to punish myself by suffering in pain?"

Like me, you'll probably deny it, but it does have some truth to it. Misery loves company, right? It was a start, and that is all it takes to make a change. You are worthy of self-care and feeling good.

Later, I had a cranio-sacral treatment (a spinal energy realignment technique) with my practitioner, which really helped open up my body and relieved a lot of stress. I went for walks with friends, did grocery shopping, joined the gym's "Silver Sneaker's" program for seniors, biked with my daughter and felt better. There are many other activities that can be chosen depending on the individual's interest.

Self-care is your friend — just choose it!

Two and a half years after the loss, I am working with a local chiropractor, Dr. Daniel Wilson in Cornelius, NC, who developed a long-term plan of care that has led to significant improvement in my mobility, decreased pain and ease of participating in activities of daily living. I can now walk up and down stairs normally instead of one step at a time. I can sleep without back or hip pain. I can walk for two miles without distress...and so much more. No more sporadic quick-fix trips for me — I'm sticking to my plan!

Also, take time to sit quietly and think about your circumstances and how you feel. Talking to others may be helpful; sometimes talking to a professional may be needed. Another strategy is to keep a journal, writing down thoughts and feelings as you process through the loss. I address this in a separate section.

Sleep is not on good terms with broken hearts.
It will have nothing to do with them.

— Christopher Pike, Author

Getting adequate sleep and rest is another way to take care of yourself physically and mentally. Sleep was a challenge at first, so I took naps whenever I felt like it. Sometimes, I would like to have retreated into a coma and disappeared for a while. I had to laugh at myself. *You know that's not happening. There's too much to do.*

It's good for you to know this "coma" thought occurs. It's normal. Just "don't do it."

SLEEP CALLS TO ME

Sleep calls to me as my day ends
And wants to be my long-lost friend.
But I hold off succumbing to
A peaceful slumber though wanting to,
Give in to rest and lay my head
On a plump down pillow —
Ahh, that's the best!

First I turn right and then turn left,
Unable to find a spot to rest.
My eyes still open and mind abuzz
As I fret about what is and was.
So, I try again to build my nest
In a bed as soft as any I guess.

But sleep won't come for me tonight
And I willingly give up the fight.
So I calm my mind and say my prayers
And before I know it I'm unawares.
Then morning comes and I'm confused
As sleep has played it's final ruse!

Cheryl A. Barrett, 11/24/2017

The mind continues to replay hundreds of events, memories, and all the "I wish" thoughts that torment your nights. So, you cry yourself to sleep, or you go sleepless, or at least not remembering if you fell asleep or not. This too improves over time.

What helped me is that I kept on a normal schedule and continued to use a sleep CD that I had already used for a long time. Only under this new set of stresses, I had to sometimes replay it two, three, or even four times. The normalcy of this was very comforting. However, I needed to change the usual CD I used while my husband was alive to another one of my favorites with soothing tones for Chakra balancing. The old one elicited memories of him when I played it each night and he was sleeping beside me. Making this change worked much better.

I also visited my doctor, who offered me "something for sleep" if I needed it. A generous offer and sometimes helpful; however, I chose to forgo this option. It is worth consideration for temporary relief, but only under a doctor's care. Sleep is often elusive when it is quiet and you are alone lying in bed — your mind actively replaying and reliving events while you judge yourself harshly. This creates even more pain and sorrow. How to deal with this is unique to the individual.

My self-care was to stop worrying about "not getting enough sleep" and instead to find something to do while I was awake. When I started rehashing events, I wallowed in self-condemnation for a while. Then, I just said, *Cheryl, stop beating yourself up. You weren't perfect. Get over yourself. Think of something good, happy, positive and get a grip.*

Well, if you keep telling yourself this, it works and you feel better.

Maybe you still won't sleep better for a while, but you will feel less stressed. Sleep will eventually happen. Give yourself time to adjust.

AFFIRMATIONS:
- I nourish my mind and body.
- I breathe deeply and fully and relax my body.
- I get the sleep I need every night, and my body appreciates how I take care of it.

Plan Self-Care Activities for YOU

For those of you who struggle with guilt regarding self-care, answer this question: What greater gift can you give to those you love than your own wholeness?

— **Shannon Tanner,** *Worthy: The POWER of Wholeness*

Self-care is the best way to replenish your mind, body and spirit. Most, if not all, of us are givers in varying capacities. We give our time, our money, our expertise, and our presence generously to others on a daily basis. Yes, it's important that we give to others. But, we must also give to ourselves, which includes accepting care from others. Not only is it important, I believe that it is essential to our wellbeing.

Think of how you sometimes feel at the end of a work day — frazzled, tired, hungry and looking forward to more giving of yourself when you get home. You are in a constant state of stress that can have a negative impact on your being. If you do not de-stress, you will implode.

Have you ever considered telling someone, "I need some ME time" or "I need a time out"?

And if you have, did you feel guilty, selfish, and undeserving? Of course, you did, and I used to too. Get rid of these negative thoughts and turn yourself around! You need to care for yourself so you can better care for others. What's the alternative? You wear out and there is nothing left to give. Your resources are depleted.

So, the first thing I would like you to do is repeat this sentence every day: **"I am worthy of self-care, and I choose to plan a 'me time' schedule."**

It is even more powerful if you stand in front of a mirror and say this to yourself, as it gives the words a sense of reality while you talk to yourself in the mirror. You may feel silly doing this, so enjoy the laugh — just do it.

Choosing self-care may be stressful at first if it's a new behavior for you, so take small steps and allot 15 - 30 minutes for a self-care activity daily. The next important thing to do is to educate your family on your need for self-care and to set limits. This is also an opportunity to teach your family by example of the importance of self-care.

Plan to do one self-care activity focusing on replenishing your mind, body, and spirit. The choices can range from free to expensive and depend on your desires. If money is an issue, choose something simple like taking a walk in nature or taking a bubble bath or salt bath with candles nearby. Don't forget to put a **"Do Not Disturb"** sign on the bathroom door and leave the cell phone somewhere far away.

Here is one of my self-care examples. My daughter made the appointment for me at a local spa. I spent two hours at this spa: one hour for a total body massage and one hour for a facial. I had never done this before and felt out of place, but I did it. What a wonderful feeling the massage was — caring hands gently gliding over my tired, stressed body. The benefit here was not only the immediate caring feeling, but afterward, the release of trapped stress toxins that were worked out of my tissues. The facial was also wonderful and included a hand and foot massage. Something strange happened during the facial experience, I started crying for no reason when my attendant was out of the room. I did not try to figure it out, I just let it be. I left the spa feeling cared for and renewed, as well as grateful to my daughter for such a wonderful gift.

Self-care activities can be anything that makes you feel good, feel peaceful, feel cared for, and feel relaxed. Some call them guilty pleasures. I consider them survival skills for living…no room for guilt there. Don't suffer, choose self-care!

Use the **Self-Care Activity Worksheet** on the next page to create and plan your strategies for caring for yourself. Follow the instructions included here as a guide for success.

In each box, write a few things that you consider self-care that you can accomplish daily. There are two additional boxes to write items of your choice. Once you have listed your ideas, put an amount of time next to each one that you are willing to commit to the activity. Then make a choice to do one activity…and do it. Once you have written down your choices, you have a better chance of follow-through. Remember that you deserve and need this self-care to be your best for others, as well as yourself.

You may start your self-care activities without revealing them to others at first. But remember, you can also include your family and/ or friends by educating them to your needs. Do whatever meets your requirements. This will take practice if you are a novice to self-care. You may find a friend who is willing to be your accomplice in self-care! Don't be bashful, just ask.

AFFIRMATIONS:
- I honor myself and take care of all my needs.
- I love every cell of my being.
- I take time out for myself to restore my mind, body and spirit.

Self-Care Activity Worksheet

Below is a table with several items identified for self-care. Create your own copy of this format and use the instructions in this section to create your self-care plan.

Physical Exercise:	Periods of Rest:	Sleep:
Massage:	Eating:	Relaxation:
Humor:	Other:	Other:

Visit the SPCA or Hug Your Pet

Animals are such agreeable friends — they ask no questions, they pass no criticisms.

— George Elliot

Talking to the animals and petting them has been proven to be therapeutic under normal circumstances, but during times of stress, pets are an invaluable asset in the recovery process. They offer unconditional love — and more. As you lean toward them, they move toward you, some more hesitant than others due to their experience with humans. Yet, they wag their tails as you tell them your tale of woe; they lick your hand as you pet them or scratch their fur, making eye contact, seeking solace in each other's presence. Those who already have a pet know this. Those who do not have a pet can still experience this feeling…as I did: just take a trip to your local animal shelter.

The thought to visit the local SPCA was not unusual for me. I have donated old towels, sheets, and newspapers on a regular basis in the past — always taking time to walk among the dogs in their cages and say hello. Although there were also many cats awaiting adoption in their separate section for those preferring these fluffy pets, I have always been drawn to dogs.

On one of these visits to drop off a bag of newspapers, I met Daisy, a lonely Shih Tzu sitting in her dark and secluded cage in the back area of the building. The only source of comfort for her was the small, old, tattered rag upon which she sat.

I talked to her: "How are you doing there? Are you as lonely and scared as I am?"

Of course, I did not expect an answer. But it was good to give voice to my thoughts of grief, loss, and sadness that needed to have someone listen to them in silence, without telling me how I should feel and what I should do.

Listening skills are often undervalued, but are powerful support elements to comfort those grieving. Daisy gave me her undivided attention as I came closer. Although wary at first, she came to the front of the cage so I could pet her. I peered into her eyes and noticed that the eyes looking back at me resembled the same sad, lonely eyes I saw reflected in my mirror every day. I felt a connection between us. I wondered if she felt what I felt, as I started to relax a bit. I talked to many of the dogs that day. In fact, that day I talked to *all* the dogs, large and small. Below is a photo of another lonely dog I chatted with who listened intently to my woes.

I felt good when I left. I hope Daisy felt some comfort from our visit, too. So, why didn't I take Daisy home with me? I would have liked to — it just was not the right time.

A pet deserves much more than being just a Band-Aid for the emotional distress of my grief and loss. I already had enough responsibility, distractions, and emotional chaos, with all my energy focused on just "getting through each day." If you are thinking of adoption, take a moment to evaluate your needs and choose a pet that connects with you and your needs. Some pet shelters offer the opportunity to take a dog you are interested in for a walk in a fenced-in area. When thinking of adoption, be sure this is right for you. You are making a long-term commitment when you choose to have a pet.

Another time, I visited my friend, Anne, at her home. She had both a cat and dog. I took just one step into her home, and her pets immediately sought me out. They kept close by my side, in my lap, or nuzzling me the entire visit. I was a magnet of emotional negativity drawing the positivity of pet energy toward me — whoosh!

Yes, animals seem to sense what I now call "disturbances in the force," human emotions, whether happy, sad, lonely, angry and so on. Dogs look you in the eye, wag their tails, and quiver with excitement when they see you. They offer themselves to you unconditionally. You cannot escape their undivided attention as their love and affection gushes forth.

My response to them was similar — spontaneous and caring. I smiled back at them, even though I felt I had no reason to smile. I talked to them, even though my mind was still telling me to keep silent so I would not scream or hurt others with my words. And I shared my loving caresses…petting and hugging them, even when I thought I had no more love to give. **Pet therapy in action!**

Pet therapy has always existed, rarely studied or validated. Lately, much research has been done on the therapeutic aspects of pets, validating benefits to one's health and wellness, now accepted by mainstream health and wellness practitioners.

Today, pets in a variety of settings bring joy and caring to those in need. Therapy dogs visit nursing homes and other such facilities to interact with residents and provide the opportunity for emotional connection and healing touch. You can see the delight and joy in the residents' eyes, watch their hands reaching out to touch and pet the dog, notice the soft words spoken. A pet can provide companionship for elders living alone. Anyone who has a pet can provide testimony as to how they are comforted by their pet's presence: these companion animals keep their owners company, give them a reason to live, and can even warn them of intruders.

No wonder you feel so much better with a pet of your own or a pet shared by a friend or family member. I still visit the SPCA on occasion to talk to the dogs.

A neighbor, Ben, has shared his dog with me many times by inviting me to his home. He prepares the dog for my visit by saying: "Cheryl's coming."

Ben says his dog dances around the room in anticipation and then waits by the door or front window anticipating my visit. I do love this anticipated attention. When I come in the door, she is all aquiver on the top step, watching me closely. She dances around me when I get to the top of the stairs — while looking directly at my face and joyfully wagging her tail. I feel so welcomed and appreciated, my spirit renewed. I return this joyful energy, talking to her, petting her, and letting her perch on my lap…such special moments. I wish for you to experience them yourselves.

Remember, you do not need to own a pet to experience the benefit of this comfort. Just take a trip to the SPCA. You can also visit your friends who have pets and want to share their comfort with you. They are waiting for you to ask. So, don't wait, just ask and reap the benefits like I did!

AFFIRMATIONS:

- I feel the comfort of pets as I hug them, look into their eyes, and see their excited expressions when I am near.
- I value the special qualities of pets' unconditional love.
- I am grateful for those who share their pets with me.

Acknowledge Guilt and Regret, then Move On

Every man is guilty of all the good he did not do.

— Voltaire

Guilt and regret are two powerful feelings that descend upon those suffering the loss of a loved one. You find yourself dissecting the events prior to the loss, looking for things you did wrong that may have led to the loss, things you did not do, or things that you perceived you missed that led to the loss event. I did it, others have done it, and you will too when your time comes.

However, this does not mean you must be trapped in guilt and regret. Remember that hindsight is worthless and only causes anxiety, increased stress — and can lead to depression (which is discussed in a later section). Dwelling on guilt and regret immobilizes you in the past events and keeps you from living in the present.

Often, you keep your guilt and regrets locked inside while you relive events repeatedly. I am sure that you have heard some say: "You need to share your feelings at a time like this, and you will feel much better."

"Right," you reply, "that's easier said than done."

Some people say this and mean it. Maybe they have personal experience and truly relate to what you are going through.

Some people say this because it is expected, an automatic response appropriate for the occasion, learned behavior from their experiences.

Other people say this and are so sorry they did. They happen to be at the right time and the right place when you spew forth such painful memories that they are not prepared to hear.

How do you sort out what to do when overwhelmed with grief and loss? Take a few deep breaths to calm and relax, then go with your gut response. Some things are so personal, however, that you have guilt or regrets about revealing, things that would make you feel you were betraying your now-deceased partner and exposing your vulnerability. It's fine to keep some thoughts private. Share what you want, when you want, and to whom you want.

It will all work out.

Have a care when sharing with others the "what ifs" and the "I should haves" associated with guilt and regret. Although some will listen to you and provide caring, I found it made others very uncomfortable. Some won't really listen to you; instead, they immediately dismiss your feelings by telling you that you did your best, not what you really want to hear at first. You are looking for positive support and comfort. You just want someone to listen.

Keep in mind that they are having their own issues with the sharing/feeling process too and may not realize it. So, be understanding and patient with them, even though your brain may be screaming, "How do they know what you did was your best?" "Who are they to judge?" "What do they know?"

Again, take a few breaths to calm and relax. Things will really ease up over time…as you gain perspective. Screaming into a pillow, crying, praying, meditating, or other coping strategies may be valuable — I have used them ALL.

Guilt is anger directed at ourselves at what we did or did not do.

— Peter McWilliams

Caution! Don't get stuck in guilt, self-blame, or rehashing negative aspects of the experience. This will torment you, adding to your stress, creating havoc among mind, body and spirit. It's okay to think about each instance of guilt and regret. Write them down if you must and look at them in black and white. Try to accept what you did and did not do, one item at a time. Forgive yourself and let it go — then forgive yourself and let it go again…and again if you must.

Believe me, forgiving oneself does not happen overnight — it takes time. Later, you will realize that you really did the best you could at the time and under the circumstances. Forgiveness is talked about in another section, as well.

My daughter and I talked and shared our thoughts:

- Did we miss something?
- Could we have prevented this?
- Why did we not know?
- What do we do now?

Talking allowed us to bring our fears and thoughts into the open and work through our guilt. We clarified and verified each other's feelings. I look back every now and again and still spend some time pondering these questions and seeking answers.

Some questions have no answers. I know now and accept that I cannot change the past. I am thankful for the time my husband and I had together. I focus on all the great things we did together.

This is important, so I will repeat it. **I still circle back to regrets and guilt now and again, even though I know I cannot change the past and I have forgiven myself.**

To overcome the feelings of guilt and regret I wrote on pieces of paper some things that made me remember my husband. I did this over Christmas, four months after his death to "remember" and keep him with me. Eleven months later, I looked at them for the first time and with much emotion pouring forth. Tucked in a red Christmas bag with a gold bow were small pieces of folded paper that included:

- special words he created that had only meaning for us ("gie-sel stacks" for purple-stalked flowers we used to see along the roadside);
- special places we visited (Cedar Point amusement park in Ohio, where we rode nine rollercoasters in one day);
- special gifts he gave me (a dog that walks and sings, "I really love the way you walk");
- all the thank-you's he gave me for things I did for him (some-times this annoyed me);
- his smile (one of us would start the smile, then the other would sense it and look and smile back from the soul);
- a favorite quote of his ("I really like beer.");
- his humor (hiding in closets to jump out and scare me or my daughter);
- his love of horses (he took me to racetracks from the East Coast to the West Coast) and so many more.

These notes helped me stay connected to him as part of my life and reinforce all the positive experiences we shared. I began to let guilt and regret go so I could make room for all the best of memories to shine. I encourage you to do this too.

Grief is not as heavy as guilt, but it takes more away from you.

— Veronica Roth, Author

Movies I watched a few times dealt with grief, loss, guilt and regrets allowed me to immerse myself in these emotions. Maybe not the best thing to do, but it was therapeutic for me. I looked at these movies anew through eyes of one who now had experience:

1. *Meet Joe Black* (Anthony Hopkins, Brad Pitt) — This mov-ie dealt with dying, death, and rebirth. It demonstrated the

impermanence of life and that it has a natural end — death. It reminded me what is important in relationships — love. I always cry during this movie, yet it makes me feel better. I want to do a better job at relationships now, to make a conscious effort to care, to listen and to wish everyone the best.

2. *Hope Floats* (Sandra Bullock; Harry Connick, Jr.) One of my favorite movie tear-jerkers. I love the story, the pain and suffering demonstrated by Sandra that occurs side-by-side with the mother's optimistic outlook. One scene I remember clearly is when her mother dies and Sandra says, "Not now, momma, not now." That is just how I felt when my husband died in bed next to me: "Not now, Fred, not now." Watching this movie helped me face the reality of death and the emotions associated with death — but even more. If I choose, I could open my heart and let hope float up…renewing me, too. There are many other scenes in the movie that provide insight into the journey through life.

I love this quote from a scene in the movie:
Beginnings are scary.
Endings are usually sad.
But it's the middle that counts the most.
You need to remember that when you find yourself
*   at the beginning,*
Just give hope a chance to float up and it will.

After a death, your journey together with your loved one has ended, but another journey lays ahead of you. I encourage you: take steps to let go of the grief, sadness, guilt, and regret…embracing hope in the new beginning, though you may feel scared. This is hard work, I kid you not — but well worth the effort. Now it's your turn to create a guilt and regret resolution list for yourself and your future:

- places to go,
- people to see,
- movies to watch,
- books to read, or
- any activity that helps you to resolve these negative emotions and lift your spirit.

See the next page for a form to use or just make your own list. Take another step to happiness — **SMILE — you are loved!**

AFFIRMATIONS:
- I give myself permission to change.
- I accept myself for who I am.
- I know I cannot change the past.
- I am kind to myself.
- I accept that I am on a journey of change that will result in new opportunities.

Resource Lists: Books and Movies

Provide Feelings of Release, Catharsis (Crying), Experiential Grieving

Write down titles of movies or books that you connect with to experience shared feelings of loss and grieving. They usually provide a look at the journey through grief and loss and provide a sense of — HOPE — for personal use.

Books	Movies

Embrace Forgiveness

The moment you truly forgive, you have reclaimed your power from the mind. Non-forgiveness is the very nature of the mind, just as the mind-made false self, the ego, cannot survive without strife and conflict. The mind cannot forgive. Only you can.

— Eckhart Tolle, *The Power of Now*

I looked in the mirror one day. I saw a sad, lonely. and broken woman looking back at me. Her head tilted downward, shoulders slumped in defeat, eyes swollen and red, hair a mass of tangles and clothing wrinkled and worn.

What happened to me, I thought? *I used to be happy, neat, active and loving.*

A voice inside me said, *you deserve what you look like and how you feel because you could have done better.*

I felt like I got slapped in the face with the realization that I was carrying around a heap of guilt and regrets, unable to forgive myself for many things. Why should I forgive myself? Surely, I should suffer — and suffer I did, until I learned to forgive myself and my husband.

Yes, forgiveness was the hardest task for me in the process of healing my wounded spirit from the loss of my husband, Fred. Forgiveness was the step that took the longest.

At first, I was angry about much that related to my loss: that I was now alone, that I regretted things I should have said or done, that I may have missed something that could have changed or prolonged his life…and many more emotional issues. A constant bombardment of negative thoughts became roadblocks on my journey through the grieving process and healing.

I felt like a victim of a tragedy — and indeed I was a victim, the lone survivor of the loss of a loved one — the other half of *me*. However, I realized that I did not have to remain a victim. I could choose to become whole again through the act of forgiveness.

It's very important to recognize that forgiveness is the voluntary act in which you willingly let go of a perceived wrong toward you that elicits feelings of anger, resentment, or other negative emotions. You feel righteous in your position of being wronged and you want to hold on tight to this feeling — waiting for the one who wronged you to "make it right."

Well, this making it right could happen, but don't hold your breath waiting. There are complications with this thinking:

- the person who you feel has wronged you may not know how you feel;
- the person may not be available to apologize to you (death is an example);
- or the person may not care how you feel.

I am sure you can think of other scenarios. Whatever the reasons for the negative emotions, if they are left unresolved, you will suffer in a state of un-forgiveness.

Let me assure you, until I was able to move through the forgiveness process, I was suffering big-time.

Remaining in the state of un-forgiveness is unhealthy. It can create chronic anxiety, harming the mind/body/spirit and self-esteem:

- Your **mind** is operating at high speed, processing and reprocessing the negative emotions that steal your joy and block your path forward.
- Your **body** is following the mind's lead dealing with the effects of all this negativity: increased tension in muscles, possible increased blood pressure, insomnia, overeating or under-eating, etc.
- Your **spirit** feels defeated, unworthy.
- Your **self-esteem** plummets to depths you never experienced.

Not good feelings for sure, as I can attest to the constant anxiety and feeling of defeat.

However, I did not give up hope.

Working through this process of forgiveness worked well for me regarding grief, loss, and anger. I did not think of forgiving anyone right away. I was wrapped up in the negative emotions and thoroughly immersed in my own suffering. I felt righteously justified in my beliefs and held onto them…feeling a sense of power. Over time, however, I became aware of how these negative emotions were eating away at me and taking up so much of my time.

I realized that the first step in the forgiveness process, awareness, allowed me to acknowledge my negative thoughts and feelings that were feeding my suffering and keeping me a victim. Next, I came up with the list of questions shown below, and I started exploring the answers. This process allowed me to take back control and enhance the clarity of the real issues. Finally, I forgave myself and let it go.

Here are some questions I asked myself that may help you also:

- Who am I unwilling to forgive?
- What did they do that hurt me and made me develop these negative feelings?
- Why am I letting this person have any control over me and cause distress to my mind/body/spirit?
- How can I forgive the wrong I perceived?

Take your time. Find a quiet place to reflect on these questions. Write them down for reference. You will be surprised how you feel after doing this. It took some time before I could forgive my husband for dying and leaving me to continue on alone.

And so, the process began.

Little by little, I started to deal with my feelings and need for forgiveness. I started asking myself:

- *Who was I not willing to forgive?* The answer — my husband.
- *What did he do that hurt me?* The answer. — he died, left me behind to continue alone and created guilt and regrets.
- Why *did I let this control my mind/body/spirit?* The answer — I needed to keep the connection to him no matter how much it hurt me.
- *How can I forgive the wrong I perceived?* The answer — I do not want to yet.

As I became aware of my responses to these questions, I decided to forgive him for leaving me. After all, he did not die on purpose to hurt me. Arriving at this place of forgiveness took much time. It was hard work to let go and move forward.

Forgiveness of self, I found, was a much harder task to do than forgive someone else. I still asked similar questions:

- *Who was I not willing to forgive?* The answer — me.
- *Why did I let myself feel un-forgiveness?* The answer. — because I felt like I was somehow responsible for the loss.
- *Did I miss health clues that I could have done something about?* The answer — I'm a nurse and should have noticed. I flagellated myself regularly for this.
- *Did I show how much I cared and loved him?* The answer — I regretted not telling him I loved him or hugging him more. I regretted spending so much time working and so little time with him — and more.

Forgiving myself took much longer, but it did happen. I must admit that even after I forgave myself, I slipped back into moments of un-forgiveness. It happens. Just forgive yourself again. **Don't give up!**

Remember, we are born to be spiritual and compassionate human beings. Embrace your spirituality and heart's compassion to forgive yourself for the perceived errors and feelings of negativity — one step at a time. Let go of the emotional negativity and dare to open your heart to receiving the blessings of peace and comfort. You did the best you could at that time, in that place, with that person.

YOU and I still have our own journeys. We must move forward to live lives filled with joy and love. This takes time. Be kind to yourself. Fully embrace forgiveness toward the one you feel wronged you AND toward yourself — it is the right thing to do.

Love yourself enough to forgive yourself!

AFFIRMATIONS:
- I forgive myself for what I think I have done wrong.
- I love myself for the person I am yet to become.
- I forgive my past and embrace every positive moment of the present.

Recognize the Humor in Situations: Laugh Alone or with Others

When the woes of existence beset us, we urgently seek comic relief.
The more emotions we invest in a subject, the greater
it's potential for guffaws.

— Patch Adams, MD

There is nothing funny about your journey through grief and loss — or is there?

Humor is not something you seek out when you are going through grief and loss. However, it is ever-present waiting to be invited back into your life. Humor pushed its way into my healing journey early and has eased my heart's pain on many occasions. Only you know when the time is right to embrace humor again and experience its healing power.

At the last viewing I attended, I was standing apart from others in the back of the funeral parlor, observing everyone. I saw the grieving widow bravely standing next to the coffin, dressed in black with sadness and grief evident on her face, her eyes staring straight ahead, and her hands trembling. The smallest thing set off a crying spell for all to witness. Someone placed a hand on her shoulder for comfort and another put tissues in her hand. I looked around and saw friends, family, and others who came to support her anxious, yet wary about how to help.

What else did I see? Some of those who came were also crying, some were stoic and keeping a stiff upper lip, while others were smiling in conversation and even sharing a laugh or two together. They were remembering the departed person in relation to a humorous event in which there was much shared laughter — an event I too remembered and smiled.

No, they were not being disrespectful. They were sharing fond memories of their time with the departed friend. They were also using humor and sometimes laughter as a coping mechanism to deal with the situation, to ease their discomfort.

You, too, have these happy, laughable shared memories and need some relief from the overwhelming emotions of grief and loss, but are unsure what to do.

What is humor? How can it help during times of grief and loss?

Humor is a positive emotion that can diffuse the many negative emotions you are experiencing — great for stress reduction. According to many, humor is good medicine. Humor therapy has been used as a coping mechanism to help deal with life's hardships.

Seeing the humor in life sometimes makes the most sense to us. Laughter makes you smile, and those around you are infected with it. Studies have shown that the benefits of laughter include:

- improving oxygenation to the brain,
- relieving tension in the muscles,
- creating a sense of peace.

I remember my husband and I sitting downstairs in the living room one day. We heard my daughter laughing so hard upstairs that we just looked at each other and started laughing too.

No doubt you have laughed before and are familiar with the joy it brings. Can you remember the last time you laughed until your cheeks

hurt and tears flowed down your face? Were you alone in your laughter? That's okay. Or, were you with someone? That's even better —
shared laughter is awesome.

Relax and enjoy a good laugh now and again —what a relief it is!

*The art of medicine consists of keeping the patient amused while
nature heals the disease.*

— Voltaire

During the healing process you may ask yourself this question:
"Did I share laughter and humor with my loved one?"

If the answer is yes, then why not use memories of shared laughter
to heal? Remembering shared times of laughter brings a smile to your
face. It feels good.

I have many memories of shared laughter with my husband. Each
time I recall one, I see his smiling face and hear the laughter — his,
mine, and sometimes my daughter's. A memory such as this can be
triggered by intentionally recalling a shared event or upon seeing a
picture, words, or something else, related to such a memory.

For example, my daughter saw a stuffed animal in the store; its hair
was peaked at the top of its head. This was a humor-event-trigger for us
that caused us to break out with laughter. Why? This was the way my
husband's hair looked in the morning when he got up. His hair would
be plastered down on the sides and straight up in the middle: thus, we
called him "Freddy the Fin."

Such precious memories make me cry sometimes, as they can no
longer happen in real-time. But, that's OK. Sadness and happiness can
and do coexist.

New things that make you laugh can happen to you during your
time of grieving. Both my daughter and I laughed at the car break-
down situation previously described and felt relief of tensions. We
rolled our eyes and looked heavenward, saying: "Are you kidding me?"

as if talking with my husband, whom we could also picture joining us in our laughter…as we sat helpless in a car that wouldn't start with rain pouring down outside, thunder cracking, and lightning zapping through the night sky.

Burned into our brains, it's a recollection we still frequently chuckle about — one very special memory. Later, we could laugh at more and more memorable experiences we had with my husband.

Humor often relies on the difference between how things are and how they should be. It helps us gain perspective and can play a significant role in the journey through grief and loss — perhaps the one thing that helps you through a rough day. Here's a poem to make you laugh and ponder the duality of laughter and sadness.

LAUGH

Don't make me laugh I've often said,
I'll pee my pants or wet my bed.
So I stay still and keep real stiff
As I cross my legs and do not shift.
Yet it creeps forth unwillingly
This joyous sound of laughing glee.
Is laughter worth the price of pee?
Yes, I whole-heartedly agree.

Don't make me laugh I've often said
I need my sorrow, pain and dread.
So deep inside I seal up tight
As I grasp each piece with all my might.
But then a whisper of mirth I hear
Bursts through the heartache and the fear.
Against my wishes, I smile and laugh.
Yes, laughter will be my epitaph.

Cheryl A. Barrett, 11/15/2017

Do you have such memories that make you both laugh and cry? Share these memories; write them down — enjoy those precious moments again and again!

What other things can you do to create laughter? Just ask yourself what made you laugh in the past? Those memories are waiting for you to remember.

During a stress management course I took a few years ago, we each had to choose a project to complete. The project I chose was a "Tickler Notebook," a collection of various items that you think can stimulate laughter. I filled it with so many things that made me laugh: comics, pictures, sayings, poems, greeting cards, photos from a movie and many more.

It so happened that a colleague of mine was diagnosed with breast cancer and was going through this stressful life event. I made a copy of the Tickler Notebook and a co-worker of mine, Annmarie, added her beautiful butterfly photos with words of encouragement on each. We arranged this special Tickler Notebook and presented the final project to the colleague, hoping to bring her a little laughter and hopefully positive benefits. She was overwhelmed with our gift and shared her appreciation telling us how much she laughed.

Two activities below that I did were helpful to me: they got me out of the house, focused my attention on something other than my gloomy internal thoughts and stimulated laughter — even laughter at myself.

I went to the greeting card section of my favorite store and lingered for a while reading the cards. Choosing cards at random first, then picking the ones that were humorous and made me laugh. At first, I chuckled silently and then the chuckles became more audible. Sometimes, others looked up and smiled at me, and we became comrades in shared fun. What could be better than sharing laughter? I have even done this with a friend who was feeling down. It will cheer them up too. I lingered in the greeting card section before my loss too, so had it in my stress management tool box to use.

The second activity made others laugh at me — and that's OK.

I found that staying in the card section for a while, organizing them into their proper places, was fun and soothing — but this also created chuckles from others. Sometimes, they joined in the fun, and we did an outstanding job of organizing the cards into a very neat display. We also shared some life experiences, sharing comfort and laughter. And, we gave the store worker an anonymous gift — another thing to smile about.

For those of you susceptible to obsessive behavior: be careful, as the organizing fun event can migrate and mutate to other areas of the store: for example; arranging the air fresheners according to their scents on the shelf. It still happens to me on occasion, but I've learned to deal with it, because it is something I can control when I feel out of control, sad, or lonely.

Maybe you have some secret things you do that nobody knows about…as I've revealed here. Enjoy!

When I'm down in the dumps, I often watch funny movies. Some movies stimulate emotions and bring forth laughter. You know what strikes your funny bone. You probably have a few movies that you can rely on to make you laugh. Take a moment to develop a list of the movies that make you laugh, movies that you have shared experiences with your loved one or your children…or choose new movies. Then plan some time to watch them alone or with someone else.

At first, you might have difficulty paying attention, as you are distracted by your woes. Have patience. Don't give up. You'll get the hang of it. Watching a funny movie with a friend can have the additional benefit of sharing the laughter as you watch each other's response. Remember, laughter is contagious! Here are a few movies that made me laugh and rekindled some wonderful memories with my husband that had a healing impact:

1. *Innerspace* (Dennis Quade, Martin Short, Meg Ryan) — I just loved the music, "Cupid" and "Twisting the Night Away," the latter of which played for several minutes at the end, and I danced with the music. It reminded me of music played during

my childhood, melodies that both my husband and I related to. I laughed throughout the movie, sang the old familiar songs, and felt good.

2. ***Caddy Shack*** (Bill Murray) — My husband and I watched this every chance we got. I loved the groundhog and his little dance. We both laughed and smiled at each other. Now when I see this movie, I am reminded of the good laughter we shared together. I can still laugh at it. I even have a furry groundhog that makes the same moves as the one in the movie and plays the same song. I can flip it on anytime I wish; it makes me smile and laugh.

3. ***The Other Woman*** (Cameron Diaz, Leslie Mann, Kate Upton) — My daughter and I have watched this several times and shared many laughs at EVERY viewing. It is a newer movie that only the two of us had watched together, but just the other day, I watched this movie with my best friend, who had not yet seen it, and we both laughed. We enjoyed sharing the laughter; she said it perked up her day, providing respite from her hectic pace and from obligations that had been getting her down.

4. ***The Best Exotic Marigold Hotel*** (Judi Dench, Tom Wilkinson, Maggie Smith, Bill Nighy and Dev Patel) — A movie filled with many prominent, seasoned actors had some funny moments that I laughed at and enjoyed. One thing that particularly touched me was the way they embraced life's changes, ups and downs evolving into the next phase of life's journey. They were seniors like me who had experiences like me and showed how they coped and continued their life's journey. This gave me hope.

5. ***Leap Year*** (Amy Adams, Matthew Goode) — I have watched this movie alone and also several times with my daughter. We laughed a lot. What struck me was the love story. When you least expect it, love comes your way. I remember how it was to be young and in love with my husband. We met on a blind date, and things just progressed from there. I feel blessed to have been part of his life for the time we had.

P.S. —I have watched these movies many times and will still choose to watch them in the future — hopelessly addicted to a good laugh!

Now it's your turn to create a laughter list when you are ready:

- places to go,
- people to see,
- movies to watch,
- books to read,
- or any activity that lift your spirit and tickle your funny bone.

Most folks are about as happy as they make up their minds to be.

— **Abraham Lincoln**

Make up your mind to be happy and enjoy family, friends, and the new life's journey that lies ahead. Use the form at the end of this section to make your own list. Take the first step to happiness — **SMILE — you are loved!**

AFFIRMATIONS:
- I give myself permission to laugh and find joy in everyday things.
- I use laughter to ease tension in my body.
- I am filled with positive actions.

Resource Lists: Books and Movies

Provide Feelings of Release by Laughter or Humor

Write down titles of movies that are humorous, that make you laugh. Movies you love to watch over and over. Remember, laughter is music to the soul. Laughter releases stress; you feel lighter.

Books	Movies

Beware of Anticipatory Grief

Worrying does not take away tomorrow's troubles.
It takes away today's peace.

— Unknown

Let's spend a few moments talking about anticipatory grief. It can have a significant impact on the guilt and regrets you may feel at the loss of a loved one. For those of you who are unfamiliar with this term, **anticipatory grief** describes grieving behaviors exhibited by a person regarding the "potential" loss of a loved one, before the actual death.

Anticipatory grief is a common occurrence. It can happen during an illness, an accident, or separation from a loved one (pets included). Your thoughts become focused on the "what ifs:"

- When is it (death) going to happen?
- What will I do?
- How will I manage when he or she is gone?

This behavior stimulates worry and stress, as well as distraction from the present — the time you have **NOW** to be with, and enjoy, life with your loved one.

Here are only a few examples of situations that may create anticipatory grief causing you to ponder the "what ifs:"

- A breast cancer patient has been given a prognosis of six months to live.
- An Alzheimer's patient no longer remembers who you are.
- A stroke patient can no longer communicate or has a physiologically changed appearance, no longer the loved one you recognize.
- A beloved pet has fallen ill, and there is nothing more that can be done.

I'll share a personal example from my experience. I made a deal with my husband when we married that he would work the first 10 years and I'd work the last 10 years of our time together; never thinking that might mean our separation in death at the end of my last 10 years of work.

As the end of my 10 years of working approached, I started to have anxiety and worry as to when I would lose my husband — irrational thinking, but that's a fact. He already had endured a few strokes and heart issues, so it was not a far stretch to consider death and separation.

As a little more time passed, I became more anxious and worried more — constantly anticipating an impending loss. I became very distracted and fearful. I started creating some emotional distance from my husband, foolishly thinking this would help cushion the blow of the loss when it came. I was sure it would be soon.

Imagine my surprise as I felt even worse when he did die, because my behavior of distancing from him added to my guilt after he died. Yes, the "could haves," "should haves," and "would haves" came back to haunt me. I beat myself up for creating this distance between us: I wished I had been closer, hugged him more, spent more time with him and so on and so on. I was angry that I cheated us both out of some precious moments we could have shared together. It took quite a while to come to terms with this and forgive myself.

If I could do it over again, I would have been more realistic about the 10-year scenario and not created the drama of impending death around it. I would have spent less time working and more time enjoying the gift of our life together. Worry and fear are powerful emotions that can skew our thoughts and behaviors, robbing us of joy.

When you recognize these behaviors in yourself (awareness is the key here), then you need to stop, take a few slow breaths to calm yourself. As you are doing this, replace the worry and fear with positive thoughts. Sit and do this for just a few moments. You will start to relax. Worry is about the future you do not know, and regret is about the past you cannot change. The present, however, is your gift to dwell in joy and love, sharing these gifts with others. The present is your NOW.

What's on your mind becomes what's in your life,
so think thoughts you want to see.

— **Karen Salmansohn, Author**

AFFIRMATIONS:
- I will keep my thoughts positive and put worry aside.
- I will embrace the present moments with joy.
- I abandon old habits and choose new, positive ones.

Recognize the Signs of Depression and Take Action

It is an absolute human certainty that no one can know his own beauty or perceive a sense of his own worth until it has been reflected back to him in the mirror of another loving, caring human being.

— John Joseph Powell, *The Secret of Staying in Love*

You have been experiencing a variety of emotions by now: grief, loss, anger, sadness, fear, anxiety, abandonment, and much more. Your sense of worth and belonging was joined in one way or another to the loved one whose loss you are grieving. You feel sad and may have what are called "the blues." You may have lost interest in things you usually enjoy.

Beware, depression lurks in the shadows of grief and loss, waiting to pounce and feed on your weakened state, leading you into the deeper waters of despair and hopelessness.

You, like many others (myself included), can and often do experience mild depression during stressful times such as this. For many, this passes within a short time. On the other hand, some find this stressful time too overwhelming to deal with and do indeed slip into the grips of depression.

Don't do it; don't slip, I say. Be strong, join ranks with those willing to support you and help you through this darkness. Ask for help whether it be family, friends or a skilled professional.

You can win over depression! I did, twice so far.

When I was a young woman with a three-year-old child, I exhibited most of the signs/symptoms of depression. I was alone in an apartment all day, had few friends, and I felt lost. I retreated into myself until I did not know what was real or what was fantasy. Nobody knew. I thought nobody cared.

One day I was in a bookstore, looking at books on depression. Yes, I knew I was depressed. No, I did not ask for help. I found a book, *How to Win Over Depression*. I read it and practiced what it said would help.

I conquered depression, but it was hard work. The most important lesson I learned was to act — get up and get moving, doing something every day! I still remember this time. It has provided me with the strength to face depression yet again. So, when I lost my husband and started to become depressed, it was easier to recognize the patterns and force myself to walk away from the grips of depression…one step at a time.

This is what I think you need to know to help you escape the clutches of depression. Keep in mind that you may not be ready to act on the information below, but it will serve you well when the time is right.

- First, understand what depression is.
- Second, know what symptoms of depression you have.
- Third, evaluate your resources.
- Then using this information, create an action plan to loosen the grip of depression and reclaim your life.
- Finally, and most importantly — you need to **ACT!**

So, what is depression? Commonly known as the doldrums or the blues, depression is a feeling of sadness that creeps into your mind, body and spirit — sometimes in overwhelming waves crashing around you. But, other times, depression is a stealth invader creeping forward to overtake you a little at a time, thus, limiting and interfering with your ability to move forward on your journey to recovery from the trauma of loss.

Depressed, you feel a sense of helplessness and/or hopelessness. You want to give up and give in to all the negative aspects of the emotions you are experiencing.

You may have had a bout or two of depression. You may know someone who has experienced depression. Think about your previous experience or theirs:

- What did it look like?
- What did it feel like?
- What helped to break free of depression's grip?

Answers to these questions could help you. Building on past experiences and successes provides confidence, strength, and resilience!

The signs and symptoms of depression are red flags that you need to pay attention to! They are varied and may include some of the following:

- withdrawal from or decreased interest in the usual social activities,
- social isolation,
- feeling worthless or guilty,
- trouble sleeping or sleeping too much,
- unkempt appearance (personal hygiene and dress),
- crying a lot,
- difficulty concentrating, thinking, or remembering,
- eating too much or too little (varies depending on a person's usual coping behavior),
- decrease in physical activities,
- feeling a loss of energy, being tired all the time.

If you have some of these signs and symptoms, you may be experiencing a bout of depression. You may not recognize that you are depressed, but someone else may identify this problem and either gently tell you, or just outright broadside you, with this unwelcome revelation. Either way, you have two choices: listen to them or ignore them.

Pay attention to what your family and friends are saying to you. You might not like it. You might not believe it. Just trust that they have your best interests at heart. Embrace their loving help. You will be happy you did.

Admitting you are depressed is hard. It reveals your vulnerability at a time when **YOU** feel that you need to be strong. If you are demonstrating any of the behaviors listed above, how strong are you really? Asking for help is not a sign of weakness!

So, make a choice to do something, but what something? First, talk to someone, a friend, a family member, or perhaps a physician visit is needed. Open your arms wide to accept help; depression likes its new home — **YOU!** Get as much support as you need.

If you have other obligations — such as work, children etc., depression has a harder time to dig its claws into you: as they claim a good deal of your attention. These responsibilities push you to get up, move and break the bonds of depression, at least briefly.

Don't be fooled, however, as depression is an opportunist lurking, waiting until you slow down. When this happens, depression pounces and digs its claws into your mind/body/spirit. Remember: you are in control. You can banish depression once again.

Some things that helped me during this time involved staying connected to others and being active. Many of the stories or topics you read in this book are really action steps for self-care which includes kicking depression off the path of your journey.

Your journey may start by doing just one thing, just one positive act…and then another and another will follow.

Just **DO SOMETHING!** Here are some suggestions that I have learned from experience that have worked for me. What works for you?

- Get up out of bed every morning and stay away from the bedroom as much as possible — it should only be used for sleep at night, but is so easy to climb back in and cuddle up again.
- Get washed and dressed in clean clothes every day — clean scent makes you feel better.
- Take a walk outside by yourself or with a friend — company eases the loneliness.
- Play music that you enjoy hearing — remember music is healing to the spirit.
- Make a date to meet a friend and keep it — commitment is action.
- Eat something for breakfast, lunch and dinner — needed fuel for the body.
- Watch a movie that makes you laugh — relieves tension and remember, it's not a crime to laugh now.
- Go to church if that is part of who you are — feed your spirit too.
- Meditate — stills the mind and opens it to unlimited possibilities. Or just sit quietly and breathe peacefully.
- Invite a friend over — they are just waiting for your call.

Some may also need the support of a physician and an antidepressant to get through this stressful period. Your doctor will help you make this decision. Others single-handedly fight depression, only to later consult a physician. How you handle depression is an individual choice as everyone has different needs. Take a firm hold of your reins: control; don't be controlled.

I had a few people, who upon their first encounter with me expressing their condolence, tell me to go to the physician and get some Xanax or Valium to help. It sounded to me as though this was their standard advice to others during loss. Surely, they did not know me very well. As a nurse, I knew I did not want anything that would numb my brain leaving me to walk through each day in a fog. I had to go to work, I had to be strong for my daughter. I wanted to experience this grief, this thread of connection still palpable between my husband and me. I wanted to remember, to honor, to be present — to bear witness to our life together. I chose what worked for me.

What lies ahead on this journey may be too wonderful to miss! Yes, keep hope alive that a wonderful future awaits you — that's what your journey is all about. Your loved one has already completed their journey, maybe too soon in your opinion. Yours is still ahead of you! This may not be clear at the beginning of your journey, but it slowly emerges and you have only to embrace it. No need to rush.

Included at the end of this section is a **Depression Action Plan**, a list of action items to choose from which will aid you to develop your own unique actions to implement for a specific time you determine. You may choose to use it or not — the choice is yours. You are in control of this journey. Dip into your toolbox of previous successful coping strategies, that have built resilience in the past, to bounce back again.

You may choose to just peek at the tool and pick an action at random and just do it. You may also choose to approach the challenge a bit more deliberately and read from the list in the Action column, put your choice of action, including how often and for how many minutes you will commit to this activity, in the second column. Then in the final column, you can write what you accomplished.

You may have attempted to do an activity and not completed it, feeling like a failure. No worries, you can try again. There is no time limit to your progress, only the limitations **YOU** put on it. Go at your own pace…keep trying. Experiment with other tools, methods or advice from family and friends.

But always remember — be kind to yourself, breathe, try to relax, and celebrate your successes!

AFFIRMATIONS:
- Obstacles are now falling away easily.
- Today is a clean slate.
- I release the need to replay situations in my mind.

Depression Action Plan

Taking action is important in dealing with depression, but sometimes just taking the first step (recognizing and taking ACTION) is the hardest. Below is a list of action items that you can choose from (or add your own to) that will help you get started regaining your life back from depression. And, yes you can do this at your own pace...but please choose to do something. You will be happy you did. It just takes time and commitment. **You can do it.**

Action I choose to do for at least _____ minutes (Start small, just one choice and add more when you are ready)	My choices for action	What I accomplished
I choose to stay physically active in some way... • walking • exercising • biking • clean out the closet • window shop at a local mall • join a gym or exercise center • dancing		
I choose to make time for activities that bring joy and happiness... • watch a movie • listen to music • do a hobby • join a quilting group • visit a garden		

Depression Action Plan
(continued)

Action I choose to do for at least _____ minutes (Start small, just one choice and add more when you are ready)	My choices for action are	What I accomplished
I choose to spend time with those who care about and can support me... • my best friend • my church group • my co-workers • my family		
I choose to practice relaxing my mind, body and spirit... • meditation • yoga • silence • prayer • mindfulness		
I choose to eat nutritional meals... • fruits and vegetables • lean meats or fish • cut down on junk food		
I can accomplish my goals by taking small steps... • ONE STEP at a time...		

Take Time to Be in "The Present"

People don't realize that now is all there ever is; there is no past or future except as memory or anticipation in your mind.

— **Eckhart Tolle**

During the grief and loss process, the beginning of your journey is focused on the heartbreak of what you lost (the past) and your fear for what is to come (the future). Daily, in (the present), you move in a fog of disconnectedness, somewhat functional, but allowing the routine of life and the expectations of others to lead you unconsciously forward.

You want to withdraw inside yourself, not move forward, but sleep and wake up after it's all over — sadly, that's not going to happen. I had these fears. What helped me was to start writing down the events happening around me, to remember things too hard to hold onto that were occurring in the present. I address these in my journal section.

At a time like this, you need to take a reality check. Try to be connected in **THE PRESENT** — just breathe. Sit quietly, close your eyes, focus on your breath, feel it flow in and out of your body — that is all. If your mind wanders, bring your focus back and follow your breath… again and again as necessary. This helps to still the mind, the first step to being in the present.

What do I mean by "being in the present?" My ideal explanation of "the present," is a breath-to-breath experience which is fleeting and ever-changing. It is neither the past nor the future...where you are currently spending much of your time struggling during your loss. Yes, we relive the past after a loss, desperately seeking answers to so many questions — many of which may remain a mystery forever. We also try to look into the future, asking other questions yet to be answered.

However, we must remember that we live in "the present," a precious gift indeed; and here, we choose to do this or that instead of something else. But what if that something else was more important, causing regrets in the future? Yes, your choices are important.

Ask yourself, "If today is all I have, what would I do?"

Here are some of my thoughts, but make your own list. These are questions I asked myself and wished I would have done differently. Now, ask yourself these same questions:

- Would you still work 12 hours a day?
- Would you spend more time with your family?
- Would you say, "I love you" more often?
- Would you hug your loved ones more?
- Would you spend less time on the computer?
- Would you try meditation?
- Would you make a bucket list?
- Would you laugh more often?

I was already familiar with "the present" and practices for being mindful of it. The following paragraphs share my awareness unfolding as I practiced connecting with "the present."

Sitting outside on the porch, only looking downward and inward like any sufferer, I felt the tension of a frown, the slumping of my shoulders pulling my head forward and downward, the drooping of my face and the sadness in my heart. My body was drowning in grief and loss.

On this one day, however, something pulled me to look up and around the area outside my back porch. I started to notice the simple things: the trees swaying in the breeze, the smell of newly mown green grass, clouds floating by, dotting the blue sky, and I heard the birds singing. I felt a little lighter — reaching out to reconnect with the world, but the suffering posture was still pulling me down. This awareness was just one step in expanding outside myself and becoming part of the present.

Then, one day riding in the car with my daughter, I looked at the distant scene before me, and I kept catching glimpses of a brightness and clarity that kept slipping away. Something stirred within me. I tried to pay attention to what I was doing: widening my eyes, taking in the periphery around me and letting my body feel the reaction. What I felt was a lightness. The muscles in my face changed.

As I widened my vision, I felt a pulling upward from my scalp. My frown slowly disappeared, and the edges of my mouth pulled up into a very small smile.

Wow! I felt myself expanding. I was becoming a part of the present and engaging in a moment-by-moment experience. I did not get the significance of this at first, but it kept happening to me until I realized that the feeling that floated up from within me was **HOPE** — finally.

I have created the exercise below from my education as a Transpersonal Nurse Coach. I am deeply grateful to Dr. Richard Schaub and Bonney Gulino-Schaub of Huntington Meditation and Imagery Center, NY, for their expertise and guidance in helping me develop a sense of peace, wisdom, purpose, and oneness. Some of my own personal grief work was done using their meditation and imagery practices, which have helped me more than I can ever say.

Here is the exercise. Try it for yourself a few times. Remember, I needed to do it several times myself. Take your time and do not rush. Your experience will be unique to you.

- Find a quiet place where you will not be disturbed.
- While sitting or standing outside, relax your body as you breathe in and out calmly and comfortably.

- Let your eyes wander over the scenery in front of you.
- Notice the details in this view: colors, shapes, smells, sensations, light and shadows.
- Continue to relax your body as you breathe in and out calmly and comfortably.
- Now, look at the same view, but open your eyes wider noticing what is also in your peripheral vision and at a distance beyond this detailed view. (Almost as if you are stepping into a new scene.)
- Take a few moments to experience this vision: feeling and sensing this experience.
- Then note how you feel — body, mind and spirit.
- Continue to relax as you breathe in and out calmly and comfortably.
- When you are ready, come back from this experience.

It is important to pay attention to how you feel in your mind, your body and your spirit. There is no right or wrong. Now, write down your thoughts and feelings.

- What did you see?
- How does your face feel?
- How do you feel?

One thing that helped me keep focused in the present was to become aware of when I was not in the present. Often, I found myself slipping into the regrets of the past and the worries of the future, making me sad and depressed. I was not aware of this at first. It appeared normal, yet all-consuming of my time and energy. Mourning my loss, my heart bled. Fortunately, over time, this happened less, but I continued to miss being in the present.

What I did that helped me was to raise my awareness by recognizing when I started slipping into the past regrets or future worries. I just said "stop" and started thinking of something positive, and focused on something I was doing in the present. This took practice and patience. I felt better when I did it. I still do it.

A very special person helped me keep focused in the present, my daughter, Bonnie. We drove to Florida for my husband's memorial ritual instead of flying and enduring the hustle-bustle of the airport scene. I am glad we did.

Going by car was a far better experience, allowing us time to be in the present for silence, talking, crying, remembering, and grieving our loss.

During this fragile time, be gentle with yourself. Give your heart permission to grieve, to feel, to remember. Grief and loss are emotions to be experienced for a limited time, but not to live in forever. So, take your time, move slowly through the process, employing healing practices and strategies along the way. **Taking time to be in "the present" is only one of these strategies.**

AFFIRMATIONS:
- I choose the contents of my life.
- Today I am able to breathe in and out and be still.
- I pay attention to how my thoughts make me feel.

Pray Every Day or Do Whatever Feeds Your Spirit

A happy heart is good medicine and a cheerful mind works healing, but a broken spirit dries up the bones.

— Proverbs 17:22

Prayer is important, your own and those of others offered in emails, snail mail, text messages, by phone or in person.

Each of us has a "higher power" that we look to, especially during troubled times. Our spiritual awareness may have started when we were young, in our later years, or even now during this tragic event that is causing us suffering and pain. The strength you draw from this spirituality is a significant component in dealing with grief and loss. There are many avenues to draw inspiration from: church membership; the *Bible, Koran, Torah* or other religious scriptures; daily devotionals by a variety of authors; TV ministries and others.

At first, you may feel angry with God for taking your loved one from you and often ask: "Why? Why? Why?"

I have found that there is no answer to this question, no matter how many times I asked…or how long I kept asking. However, while I was in this struggle, so many concerned people were praying for me with healing intent. I believe that prayer is powerful; it uplifts the spirit and soothes the soul.

If you have never prayed before, just speak from the heart, asking for comfort and peace. Positive intent is also powerful. Remember that positive thoughts attract positive thoughts and results; negatives attract negative.

If you maintain positive intent and hope along with prayer, you may feel your burden lighten as a heaviness lifts from your body, mind and spirit. This takes time to feel. You are contracted during your initial grief, your spirit broken, your awareness stunted — you are in a dark place.

Have faith. Time will lessen this heaviness. "Time heals all wounds," some say. I hated when people said this to me at first. However, as time moved forward, I became aware of when the heaviness began to lift, and I wanted this feeling to continue. **Don't give up!**

Nights sleeping in the same bed where Fred and I had always slept together, and where he died, were hard. I wanted to feel his hand gently pat my hip and say "good night" again. I still slept on my side of the bed for a long time; I would often reach across for him and feel nothing — only an empty space. Crying came first, then prayer, providing peace and release. I frequently recited the Lord's Prayer while waiting for the elusive sleep to come.

Prayer and my spiritual development helped me through this dark time. Reading *The Power of Being Thankful,* by Joyce Meyer was very comforting. This 365-day, scripture-based devotional provided me with a positive focus and a reminder to be thankful. Even though I had experienced a significant loss, that did not mean there weren't things for which to be thankful. I also watched Joel Osteen's TV ministry sermons and drew hope from his positive messages. In addition, knowing that Sister Mary, a colleague at Mercy Home Care where I worked, had added me to her convent's prayer list. It was comforting, as was knowing that many others said they would pray for me too.

Others may prefer meditation practices to connect with their spirituality. This method of stress reduction is useful to survive loss and can be used in times of any stressful event. Meditation, a focused intention done by an individual, can help raise self-awareness and provide peace and relaxation.

You can practice meditation alone, be guided by a prerecorded tape or an instructor in-person. It takes time and practice, so having someone guide you at first is most helpful. At first, you will likely have some difficulty staying focused and will need guidance. If it is too soon to try this now or it is not of interest to you, choose another coping strategy that works best for you.

PRAY

I fold my hands and bow my head
And pause to pray as I am led;
Searching for the words to speak
From a heart filled with sorrow and with grief.

I know God's waiting patiently
To hear me ask and make my plea.
"Take heart," He says, *"I am always here*
To share your burdens and your tears."

I feel His presence and take hope
For courage to go forth and cope.
For prayers are yearnings from the soul
Releasing compassion, to make me whole.

Yes, I am worthy, I am blessed
To have more prayers for all the rest.

Cheryl A. Barrett, 11/14/2017

If you are not familiar with meditation and want to try it, here is a very simple way to start. Do it for a minute or two at first.

- Find a quiet place, one that is pleasing to you — a garden, a living room, a den.
- Sit where you are comfortable and won't be disturbed.
- Close your eyes or gently let your eyelids flutter downward... as you wish.
- Put your hands on your lap and relax your shoulders.
- Breathe into your belly, then out through your lips or nose.
- Focus on following your breath as it enters your nose and travels to your belly, then follow your breath out again.

This will help to relax you. If your mind wanders to "thinking," that's OK. Just return your attention to following your breath. This is a short meditation that may be repeated as needed.

Just one thing to remember: I had a hard time praying every day. In fact, I did not pray every day. Sometimes, so mad at God, I could not pray. Yet, I also needed God and the comfort that prayer brings.

It was a struggle, this love / hate relationship with God. At first, I did pray, desperate for a connection to God for answers and comfort. Time passed. Busyness crept back into my life, and my daily prayers often lapsed.

Don't be too hard on yourself. Pray when you can and with heart and gratitude. Receive the healing benefits of prayer.

AFFIRMATIONS:
- I nourish my spirit and soul.
- I am peaceful, whole, and balanced.
- I let go of impatience, and I trust in the Creator's plan.

Keep a Journal

All sorrows can be borne, if you put them in a story.

— **Isak Dinesen,** *Out of Africa*

The quote above is from Karen von Blixen (pen name, Isak Dinesen). It was taken from her journals from which the movie, *Out of Africa,* a story of grief, loss, betrayal, promise, and hope, was developed.

Like Dinesen, writing down our thoughts and feelings provides an avenue of catharsis as well as a record of our grieving to be looked at later.

At the beginning of the grieving process, you are numb, forgetful, angry, distracted, and experiencing a host of other feelings. Love lives on…in the little things you shared, in the moments you'll always treasure: a smile, a knowing look, a private joke, a special touch. Little things make your love and memories matter so much now.

How can you keep these memories? One way is to start writing in a journal.

Journals can be tricky, however. Don't get locked into the thought, *I have to write every day.*

Just write when you feel like it or remember to do so and want to do it. Some of you might think, *oh, no, not another thing to add to my to do list.* Journaling may not be for you. It's your call.

I remember when I started writing down some of my experiences. It was October 2014, only a month after Fred died. I would have forgotten so much that happened if I had not written it down. A lot of what you are reading here was a part of my journal, a document that I kept on my computer desktop for easy access. It started with short memories, in short sentences, then grew into paragraphs; finally, I created titles for sections and so on.

Below is a very early entry from my journal. As you can see, it jumps from idea to idea. Some sentences are awkward. There is no perfection — only emotion:

The first week you feel numb, in shock about what happened, why it happened, what to do. Have little appetite. Am very sensitive and distracted. Sleep is sporadic, intermittent. Felt pressured to make lists of things needed to be done. Felt my own mortality and tried to do some preparation for my daughter in case anything happened to me. Burial cost, wishes of deceased.

Phone calls to family and close friends. Contact work for time off. Loss of male spouse made me feel more vulnerable and leery of asking strangers for help when alone. Slept in daughter's room first night, then in same bed spouse died in — difficult. Coping technique for me was to buy a few romance novels to read to keep my mind busy from thinking of this trial, but hard to read. Heightened awareness and being tuned in creates synchronicity in connections/ events that become meaningful. It is a time for loss (taken away) as well as a time for gifts (given). Devastated by loss of spouse scent and energetic presence. Felt like he was erased from ever existing.

So, what's in a journal, and how do I start one?

Journal writing is a series of recordings of events as perceived by the writer. The format can be in prose, poetry, sketches, doodles — it matters not how it is created. What's important is that it serves to increase awareness. Sometimes what is written is a painful outpouring from the heart, and other times it is just an impersonal description of events, thoughts, or feelings.

You can write in a paper journal, type in a computer document, dictate into an audio recorder, or create video recordings. It does not matter which mode you choose — whatever feels right for you. Just try it!

Do not worry about grammar, neatness or appropriate language. This is your tool for release.

I found it best not to reread what I had written immediately, because I did not know how to deal with the effects of self-discovery from this process. Occasionally, I would look back and reread a section and be surprised at the rawness of the feelings and emotions, yet awed by the emerging pattern of positive aspects here and there. Included with the anger, grief, and negative feelings were also good memories, thankfulness, even things that made me laugh.

I have included some journal writing tips from *Managing Stress: Principles and Strategies for Wellbeing* by Brian Luke Seaward, PhD, of Paramount Wellness Institute. I attended Dr. Luke's Holistic Stress Management Instructor course in Boulder, Colorado, a few years ago. Revisiting content in this book, I was surprised to discover that so many of the stress coping strategies learned in his class, I used during my journey through grief and loss. I am sharing his information about journaling with you with his permission. When, and if, you choose to start journaling, consider the following suggestions:

1. Try to identify those concerns and problems that cause the most frustration, grief, and tension that you want to write in your journal.
2. Ask yourself what emotions are elicited when these stressors are encountered: anger, fear, anxiety, sadness, abandonment, guilt, regret, or any other.
3. Allow the writing process to augment your creative process to further resolution. Just write what you think and feel.

4. Center yourself by taking a few deep breaths, and try to unwind before you begin. This helps to relax and ready you for the process.

5. Label your journal entries with the date and year, as you will want to review them at some time in the future.

6. Employ uncensorship in your writing. Write down your thoughts without editing.

7. Let your thoughts be spontaneous, free-flowing; do not worry about spelling or grammar.

8. Find a private place to write. Interruptions are distracting. You may become emotional during the process and need the privacy.

9. Your journal is private and for your eyes only.

If this activity proves to increase your distress, stop and explore another method of dealing with your stress that works for you. You may even seek out professional help. Everyone is different and one technique does not work for all.

AFFIRMATIONS:
- I write my thoughts down to remember.
- I transform negative energy into love and light.
- I no longer resist the lessons I'm learning.

Adapt to Change: Losing Bits and Pieces of Your Loved One

With everything that has happened to you, you can either feel sorry for yourself, or treat what has happened as a gift. Everything is either an opportunity to grow, or an obstacle to keep you from growing. You get to choose.

— Wayne W. Dyer, Ph.D

I became aware of how the loss of my husband was changing my life from the very beginning; however, I was numb with grief and only saw the global picture of life without him. It wasn't until much later that I really took notice of the little things that changed that made me feel like I was losing bits and pieces of my loved one.

We knew each other since I was 16 years old. *(But, I remember ogling him from afar since the age of 13. A story for another time.)* We were married for 46 years, which felt like forever to me. When you lose the presence of someone you have been so close to for so long, you experience an incredible void — a huge hole in the heart.

We were a unit, a team, best buddies, some would say we were "two peas in a pod."

We used to periodically kid each other by saying, "You're going to miss me when I'm gone."

We would gaze into each other's eyes and agree that indeed each would miss the other terribly. Saying these words…and then experiencing the loss…are two vastly different things.

The change in my sleeping arrangements was the first thing I noticed, as we always slept together. Each had a side of the bed that was "my space" to sleep.

Once Fred died, I had the whole bed to use for sleep. I felt the loss of his presence next to me, a presence that had made me feel safe and secure in the past. However, I still just slept on "my own side" for quite a while. This did change over time for me. After a year, I could and now do sleep anywhere in the bed without discomfort. These were the first pieces of being together that I felt drifting away, both physically and in my memory of shared experiences.

Lack of a partner to come home to after work was unfamiliar. He was there every day, waiting with a smile when I walked through the door. My man-around-the-house was my companion in household tasks and fixing things that broke. Now, I come home to a house devoid of male presence; a chill pervades the space.

We would watch our favorite TV shows together, and sometimes separately, as he had a love of horse racing and frequently watched the racing channel and other sports stations while I was watching something else in another room. I cannot bear to watch some of his favorite TV shows we watched together, like *NCIS* and *Diners, Drive-Ins and Dives*. Other shows we watched I continue to watch and feel OK.

I am fortunate that my daughter lives with me as I have said before. She has been a huge comfort. We have taken over these tasks, which now shifts us to making new memories, as the others formed with him become a part of the past — more pieces falling away.

His clothing was not touched for six months, but stayed safely in the armoire he claimed as his own. He often said, "The armoire is the only thing that is mine in this house." The rest of the house was attributed to me.

One day when my daughter was away, I started going through his clothes, creating piles to donate. These were a part of who he was and were of no use for me now; but, could be useful to someone else. My daughter came home in the middle of this process and helped make decisions on what to keep and what to donate. We did keep some of the items that we couldn't part with at first. We donated the rest to the Veterans Association. Yet more pieces of him, the special clothes we purchased just for him — gone!

Almost a year after his death, I had been replacing some appliances and doing some home remodeling in preparation to sell my home, and I was surprised at the emotional impact doing this had on me. I felt like I was losing more pieces of him, shared memories tied to "things" in our home.

I bought a new washer and dryer on my own for the first time and found myself wanting to ask my husband what he thought, but that was no longer possible. So, I just made the decision alone. I hated the new washer and dryer and included them in the sale of our home only months after I purchased them.

My husband was the king of spot removal on my clothes and did the laundry often, so often that I hid my clothes at times so the washing machine could get a break. When I used the replacement machines for the first time, I thought, *he's never touched or used these.* I felt I lost a connection to him. I had the same feeling when I replaced the kitchen range — losing another piece of him as another item he touched and used was gone from our home.

Part of the transition process when a spouse dies involves putting accounts into your name and removing/deleting your spouse's name from them, such as: bank accounts, new checks, car insurance if joint ownership, utility bills, IRAs and much more. If you are the beneficiary on his accounts, you will have to claim them and have them transferred to a new account with **your name only**. One by one, I was removing evidence of his existence and more bits of him and the memory of him disappeared. I felt like I was losing my identity, too.

I had been losing all these bits and pieces of memories and things we shared all along, but did not make the connection and reflect on the items above until I bought a new car. This was not a frivolous move, but a necessary one. He and I had been talking about a possible trade-in before his death, but we had never made a final decision.

As I was driving the new car home, I choked up. Tears started falling. I had just traded in the Honda that we had purchased together, drove together, and went on vacations with together. Now I was in a car he had never seen, never sat in, nor drove anywhere with me. I felt I had lost such a big piece of him. I was not expecting this. It just crept up on me. I wondered how many more bits and pieces of memories of him I had yet to lose. What would happen when I sold the house?

Yes, these emotions are strong. At first, you have only inklings of awareness that change is occurring. These first encounters do not provide much depth — only surface stimulation. You move on, distracted by other things in your life. Eventually, however, you have a big event (for me it was buying the car), and then "POW!" you awaken to the core issue. Not only his loss, but loss of items with shared meaning. It provided me the "Ah-ha!" moment, this awakening, followed by awareness of multiple connections…and then a catharsis.

This first response is somewhat distorted, due to the entangled emotions — a self-created drama of sorts. After this wave of emotional response passes, you can look at your situation in a more detached manner, helping you to make sense of how you feel. You may find how unrealistic your initial response was or how it fed your need to stay connected to your loved one and to the past. This is all good to experience, but it is necessary to work through the emotions, come to terms with the loss, accept that you are, and can continue to be, worthy of love and life.

There is only one thing you can do with all these changes bombarding you — adapt and move forward one step at a time. This process takes time, makes you feel broken, and creates a lot of emotional pain. You feel that all the things you assigned meaning to with memories connected to your loved one are slipping away, replaced by new things and new memories. This does not mean that those bits and pieces of who your loved one was or your memories together are gone too.

Your loved one will become a part of the past, but never need to be gone. Memories of my husband continue to live in my heart and will forever.

Here is a quote I found that gave me hope to move forward:

Never be ashamed about being broken, because strength is nothing but pain that's been repaired.

— **Trent Shelton**

You, like me, are in transition on a journey to fulfill your own purpose in life. Believe that your loved one will always be a part of your life in your memories, but you must go on. You can choose to let go, but keep the memories, and move forward with **YOUR** journey in confidence. You take it one day at a time as you gain strength from your beliefs, your friends, your family, and yourself. You belong in "the present" where you have yet to become all you are destined to be.

AFFIRMATIONS:
- I welcome change as a natural process of life.
- I adapt to change and move confidently toward the future.
- I release things that no longer serve me.

Memories of Loving You

I wish I'd done this, I wish I'd done that
I wish, I wish, I wish — I wish I had you back.

My tears still fall at will sometimes, and I miss you desperately.
There's not a day that goes by that I don't think of you with me.
My arms no longer hold you close and feel your heartbeat next to mine.
Some days, I feel such an awful ache that I fear I'll lose my mind.
Our lips no longer meet and greet followed by our secret smiles.
I've lost my step beside you as we walked so many miles.
Our hands no longer touch and hold onto like two best friends.
My heart a pile of broken shards, may take forever till it mends.
Our eyes no longer greet each other with a sparkle and a wink.
The magic of your laughter lost makes my spirit slowly sink.
Your voice is just a memory, a whisper heard in my sleep.
So, I call your cell phone now and then just to hear you speak.
Your manly scent I search for often is forever gone.
But for a secret stash of shirts I cling to — when for you I long.
It's lonely here without you and I can't seem to come to peace.
You were my best friend, my only love forever not to cease.

I wish I may, I wish I might…
But know the wish that is just right
Is the one that I'll be seeing you —
Just when the time is right.
We'll know that love's forever — forever, I'm alright.

— **Cheryl A. Barrett, 1/12/2016**

Moving On and Moving Through

*You've gone and left me. I didn't have a say, but I feel your
presence beside me as I move forward day-by-day.*

— Cheryl A. Barrett, Nurse Coach, Author

I'm lying on the floor of the temporary rental unit we have been staying
in for about a month in North Carolina. I am flat on my back, gazing
up at the ceiling, wondering what in the world am I doing here.

My back is acting up. I am in a lot of pain, and tears are leaking
from my eyes as the permanence of the decision to sell my home and
move is sinking in. I will be moving on to a new apartment tomorrow,
in a new state, in a new town.

I am experiencing so many conflicting emotions: sadness, frustration…and excitement, too. I feel I'm closing a door on a part of my
life, the known, and opening another door to the unknown. I feel I am
betraying my husband, leaving the home in Pennsylvania that was ours
for what seemed like forever…to make a new start, but without him
by my side.

Tears now stream down my cheeks as I cry for myself…for my past,
and for my future. I seem so lost, confused and alone, yet not really
alone — as my daughter is with me. O, God! I want to move forward,

but it's still so hard. I still grieve. I still hurt. I still want back what was taken from me. It's not fair. It's so wrong!

Why does it still hurt so much at times — this loss? I do not know. It descends upon me despite my wanting to heal. I must deal with it, move forward, but it's hard, a lonely journey, one wrought with uncertainty, with trepidation, but with hope and more yet to unfold.

I did not expect it, this overwhelming feeling of grief, to keep coming to the surface repeatedly. Yes, moving on is often a painful but necessary part of our lives. At two years since my loss, I have moved forward through the grief one step at a time building resilience and embracing the transformation occurring within me.

I have survived waves of guilt, regret, self-condemnation, loneliness, self-pity and more that have crashed over me — relentless at first, then easing up, only to descend upon me again. Still, I get bowled over with an occasional rogue wave of pain that is so intense, making me experience it again. There's nothing to do but let it come, experience the temporary discomfort, breathe, remind myself that I have dealt with this already — and then, let it go.

You may feel this way too. But, remember to be kind to yourself as you repeat the healing process.

On the third-year anniversary of my husband's death, I visited Pennsylvania, where my late husband and I lived for so long. I traveled by myself on this vacation for the first time ever. All went well, even better than expected.

The journey was not filled with painful memories as I anticipated, but one of peace and acceptance — I was surprised. I even stayed across the street from my old house with a friend without difficulty and chatted with the new owner and son.

I enjoyed riding around the same familiar territory, revisiting some of the places we went to and just remembering. It felt like closure, if there is such a thing in matters of a broken heart. I found out that "all is well" and yes, I survived and came out the other side. Whew, the Hero's Journey, complete — or is it?

It may seem like I have the answer to surviving the grief and loss process, but I am only a beginner — I still have much to learn. Life occurs around me without a care for how I am feeling. I meet new friends who do not know what baggage I carry with me. I sometimes wonder if they can see the invisible scars, the emotional pain, and the sense of emptiness I am trying desperately to hide from them and deal with on my own.

However, even now, I've met some people that I can share my story and vulnerability with who have their own tales to tell. We sit side-by-side and lean forward with ears perked, eyes focused and hearts open with compassion, as each takes a turn at telling stories of unique human beings encountering ordinary everyday life circumstances, some small and some big. Stories of endurance, stories of resiliency — amazing stories of survival!

Some materials I have read on this topic take offense at saying people "NEED to MOVE ON." They argue that you just "MOVE THROUGH" the grieving process: adapting, growing, relapsing, adjusting, remembering, reflecting, and being. I agree with this as time only softens the pain, but healing may never be complete.

Grief changes you. You are not the same, even at the deepest level of **YOU**. If you have been a "we" for a long time, you will be learning to love the new, emerging of self.

Keep in mind these following words of wisdom I have collected over time from my personal experience as well as from research and reading of others' stories of grief:

- Just because you have moved forward doesn't mean you never loved the one you lost. You cannot change the reality of your history, but you can continue to honor the memories you shared with those close to you. You cherish what you had and build new memories and experience joy again.
- Grieving is an unpredictable, gut-wrenching, and messy process full of progress and setbacks. Just when you think you have

made much progress, you can get bowled over by a wave of unrelenting grief. But you get back on your feet and keep moving forward.

- Brain fog may continue for more than a year, especially for those who react with severe shock and trauma to such an event. You are grieving and distracted. Be patient with yourself. Accept help from others.

- A sense of living two lives may permeate your grieving, as your emotions fluctuate from joy to despair. You may feel your sanity is at risk, but this will pass. No, you are not schizophrenic or losing your mind. You are healing. This takes time.

- Remember to use any coping mechanisms that have worked for you in the past to support your journey through grief and loss. However, if you need some help, consider consulting a professional. Sometimes you just need an extra boost in your recovery process.

- Celebrate memories of your loved one. Recollections are part of who you are. It's OK to celebrate your loved one's existence, to say their name and to continue to love them. This validates them and their role in part of your life.

- Ask for a hug when you need one. Ask for companionship when lonely. Offer your hugs and companionship to others in need. You have learned a lot on this journey. You have a lot to share with others who are experiencing the same emotions.

- And if someone tells you that it's time to move on and get over it, take a deep breath, stand firm and tell them that you need to heal at your own pace. Ask them to honor and support you in this stressful journey.

One of the most important things I learned while moving through the grieving process was this simple truth — just **keep moving** regardless of the setbacks and **allow time** for healing!

AFFIRMATIONS:
- I am strong and can move forward at my own pace.
- I ask for help to meet my needs.
- I will be kind to myself when I am feeling overwhelmed.
- I include self-care as part of my daily routine.

Be Prepared for a Calendar of Event Triggers

Time has no boundaries in matters of the heart.

— Cheryl A. Barrett, Nurse Coach, Author

The idea of a Calendar of Event Triggers may not cross your mind at first after the loss of a loved one, but it is none-the-less waiting for you. These events are, and have been, a part of your life for as long as you and your loved one have been together making memories. The dates on the calendar may be few or many, depending upon your history together. While you are alive, happy times are celebrated. It is a different story when a loved one is no longer present.

So, what are these Calendar of Event Triggers for you? They are times assigned to specific life events shared with one person or group that are meaningful and evoke strong memories that may result in stressful responses…from brief tears to profound sorrow.

If you are unaware of these or unprepared for the impact, they can catch you off guard and create emotional havoc. Yes, these Calendar of Event Triggers are like a switch that can turn your day from peaceful and calm to distraction, tears, and an emotional setback in your path to healing.

How do you prepare to survive these occurrences?

First, learn what your personal **Calendar of Event Triggers** may be. Such a list of personal events may include, but are not limited to:

- birthdays,
- anniversaries,
- Mother's Day,
- Father's Day,
- birthday of a child,
- Christmas,
- New Year's,
- Valentine's Day,
- Thanksgiving,
- July 4th.

These are some examples, but your unique life may include different calendar trigger dates. Other cultures may call these by different names or add more events not listed here.

Next, get yourself a calendar that extends at least one year forward from the loss date of your loved one. A year is an important timeline for you to prepare as this will provide the most comprehensive list of calendar of event triggers that will impact your healing process.

Keep in mind, however, that preparation such as this does not necessarily give you a relief from the emotional response. It may give you a head's up as to what is coming so you can be more prepared to face the triggering event on your terms: calmer, more reflective, with more gratitude or just an opportunity to grieve and honor the memory of your loved one. You may even take the opportunity to create a celebration with family or friends in memory of a loved one in association with a particular event.

Finally, as you live each day, you will experience calendar trigger events — prepared or not. There is no perfect way to go about getting through one of these. You will feel successful with some and feel like a failure with others. Remember, you are in the grieving process, and all is well.

Creating a Calendar of Event Triggers for someone who is dear to you is a wonderful gift. Not only will it help ease their stress of making one, but it will help you to prepare for and be available to support them when these event triggers arise.

The first calendar event trigger I experienced was Thanksgiving. At first, I did not even think very far ahead. Then, boom, the holiday was looming before me. We usually spent Thanksgiving, a festivity with all the trimmings, with my sister-in-law and her family. My husband loved to go there, watch some football, chat, and eat good food. This first year, however, all I wanted to do was stay home in my nest — my comfort zone. I found that my withdrawal left other relatives unsure of what to do or say, so we just let it be. I did nothing but stay home and miss the routine we had as a family. Instead of being a celebration for me, this Thanksgiving was just another day off from work…filled with sadness, crying and loneliness.

Then, Christmas was upon me. Another event that was shared with a family meal that I retreated from. My daughter and I sat at home watching TV together. Only the fourth month after my husband died, we were still somewhat numb, just going through the routines, fortunate to have the distraction of work to keep our minds busy. On Christmas, I took time to write down some positive things I remembered about our life together, and I put them in a red bag with a gold bow. It resembled a gift, and it represented what I felt were his gifts to me from the past. I put them aside for now.

In July following Fred's death, in his birthday month, my daughter and I were in Daytona Beach — his favorite place to visit. We had some sad times during the visit, remembering his loss. We went to the site where we had scattered his ashes in the ocean. We also celebrated him by going to his favorite places to walk and to eat; we drank a toast to him more than once.

Even two and a half years since my husband died, I still react to many of the calendar event triggers that have continued to cycle through the year. They are bearable now. Sometimes, I can even smile and feel happy for so many of these events that we were blessed to share. Death is part of life.

AFFIRMATIONS:

- Other people do not control my emotions; I do.
- I am at peace with what is happening.
- I transform negative energy into love and light.

Revisit Places of Shared Memories

There are moments when I wish I could roll back the clock and take all the sadness away, but I have the feeling that if I did, the joy would be gone as well.

— Nicholas Sparks, *A Walk to Remember*

Revisiting places that you have shared memories with your deceased loved one is something to delay for a bit in the grieving process. At least it was for me.

Maybe for others revisiting the usual haunts will have a more comforting effect. You need to determine this for yourself. These may be places close by such as restaurants, bars, movies, gardens, or other places you went to together. They may be vacations to special places: the seashore, the mountains, the desert, a foreign country, an amusement park…just about any place.

I found that some places were easier to revisit while others were difficult. For some, I needed more time. Others, I even marked off my list of places to go. I didn't rush the process.

My daughter and I visited places we had gone to as a threesome (father, mother and daughter) and reminisced over old memories as we made new experiences as a twosome — only mother and daughter now. We laughed, cried, ate, and drank at my husband's favorite places on our trip to Florida. We did some more when we returned home.

Revisiting some places took longer than others, such as Carrabba's Italian Grill. This was my husband's favorite place to go; he loved their linguini and clams with his favorite beer — Peroni. He said it was like *Cheers*, the TV show, to him. Everybody was friendly and happy to see him. They talked to him and shared their hopes, dreams, and new job opportunities. He always cheered the staff on in their school or careers and shared his years of accumulated wisdom with them.

I have reached out to a few of the Carrabba's staff via email to share his death and they replied with their condolences. I tried to stop by several times, but only made it as far as sitting in the parking lot, crying in the car, not able to get out and go into the restaurant. It was nine months later when my daughter and I eventually stopped by, had dinner, and got to share our loss with the manager, Eleanor, who hugged us as we shed a few tears together.

As a young couple, my husband and I invested in the water company, Aqua PA. We bought more stocks when we had more money, and the account grew. To check on this investment, we would take rides to the reservoir to view the water level — sometimes high and sometimes low.

Later when he did not drive much, Fred would ask me: "Let's take a drive past the reservoir."

We made one of these trips at his request on our last day together. He died shortly after midnight that night. After his death, when I drove by the reservoir, I would burst out in tears. Then, after a while, it was not so bad, and finally I was able to talk to him as I went by: "The reservoir is up pretty good today don't you think, Fred?"

My daughter and I go by occasionally, and we reflect on these trips, as she too has taken him by the reservoir. It's a memory I'll always treasure.

Recently, my daughter and I took a trip out West along a similar path that my husband and I had traveled in 2002, when he retired and I was on a break from a hectic job. I had lots of memories from my trip with Fred: the cities, the sights, and many other places we visited. But this time, my traveling companion was my daughter. As we rode along and visited certain sites I would say, "Your dad and I saw this or we did that and so on." Of course, we also made new memories in places only the two of us had gone. Some of the places we revisited did not prove very stressful, but a few made tears flow.

Being in Sedona, AZ, was emotionally stressful. Maybe it was the energy of the vortices or that this was a spiritual retreat. No matter, I was tense, cried at the drop of a hat, and needed time to myself. My fellow comrades at the retreat sensed my need and were very supportive and understanding. I fell asleep in a healing bed under a copper canopy with a lot of crystal energy around it, participated in drumming and singing, more drumming in a vision lodge, and was hugged and given a huge energy boost from a wonderful woman healer. I felt so cared for.

I will continue to experience shared memories of the past, including those that bring tears to my eyes and cause grief to shoot its arrow into my heart again, only to cause a twinge another time. I will also continue to experience shared memories of the past that make me smile and laugh at those wonderful times we had together. You will too.

Remember, however, we will continue to create precious memories in the present to be added to our life. Don't miss out on the opportunity to honor the past and explore the potential for the future. More memories are waiting for you to discover and experience. Put joy back into your heart.

Nothing is ever really lost to us as long as we remember it.

— **L.M. Montgomery,** *The Story Girl*

AFFIRMATIONS:
- I choose the contents of my life.
- I abandon old habits and adopt new, positive ones.
- I welcome positivity into my life.
- I will cherish old memories and make new ones.

Be Aware of Blessings and Express Gratitude

Gratitude turns what we have into enough, and more. It turns denial into acceptance, chaos into order, confusion into clarity... it makes sense of our past, brings peace for today, and creates a vision for tomorrow.

— Melody Beattie

As you read this section, you may be shaking your head and thinking that I must be deranged to tell you to be aware of blessings and express gratitude while you are deep in your grief.

And you would be right — at least in the beginning. Gratitude was not my first response to the tragedy of loss, I can assure you. I was angry at God, felt sorry for myself, and was surrounded by such darkness and despair.

This did not last long however. Moments of acceptance, clarity and peace peeked through to illuminate my heart. If you are asking how long is "long," I cannot say. You will move forward at your own pace and in your own time. As you accept the loss, you will receive new clarity of purpose and feel peace in your heart.

I remember my husband saying "thank you" often for taking him for a ride, going out to dinner, cutting his toenails or giving him a shiatsu treatment. He would say thanks so often that at times I would get annoyed. I never asked him why he needed to say it so much, but I wish that I had. Reflecting on this, I now think that I was being taught gratitude by him for even the little things.

He was such a blessing to me. These memories helped me increase my awareness, allowing me to become more open and receptive during the grieving process — to not only recognize blessings that came my way, but to embrace them and feel comforted through them.

In previous sections, you have already read some of the blessings I am grateful for: my daughter's presence and caring, the support and caring of my friends, the funeral manager's help making the process uncomplicated and anticipating my needs, the man at Home Depot who helped me with my car, the person at Chick-fil-A who gave me a gift card, all the comfort and caring I received from others and more. These were true blessings. I continue to receive many more. I am grateful for each experience.

Over the past couple of years, I have been growing in my spiritual life, learning to love more, give more, receive more, be in tune with nature, connected to the vibrations of serendipitous events surrounding me. I have looked at people I've met, even strangers, as an opportunity to help with some need they may have. Maybe they were lonely and needed someone to talk with. Maybe they needed help in the grocery aisle to reach an item on the shelf…and so on.

One day my daughter and I were out to dinner. We chose to sit at the bar. Soon, an older gentleman sat on the seat next to me. We had a few minutes of silence, then I could no longer keep quiet. I sensed that maybe he was seated next to me for a reason.

As I chatted with him, I found out that he had lost his wife to cancer about two and a half years prior. We talked about her and his family briefly. He revealed that days like this were especially hard…when he was off from work and had nowhere to go — I saw a hint of tears in his eyes as he said he gets lonely.

He told me, "They don't know what it's like for me to have lost her. They think I should have been over it by now and moved on."

He meant his family and friends. I knew how he felt. We continued to chat. I was grateful to be next to him and to bear witness to his story of grief and loss.

Each time an event like this has happened, I became more aware of the greater plan of life, a universal oneness and how we are all connected. Life and death are part of the journey. We each have a path to walk — together for a time…and alone for a time.

I absorbed this lesson of life and death when my husband, the other half of my heart, completed his life's journey and left me behind to continue my own life's journey. I had not really considered living without him by my side, where he had been for so long. *Strange*, I thought, *how we spend so much time with little thought to our inevitable mortality.*

I learned, after much struggling and the passage of time, how to be grateful for what we had together. I became able to identify many blessings experienced during that time. I thought of how different my life would have been without him. I am grateful that I loved and was loved by this special man — a blessing to remember forever.

I felt truly blessed to received so many cards, emails, and phone calls offering prayers, support and encouragement during this difficult time. It was hard to keep them in order. I did not want to miss thanking anyone for their thoughts and caring. So, being a bit of a compulsive organizer, I created a message from the heart that I sent to everyone.

My message of gratitude is included on the next page. There are many ways to perform the ritual of tracking and responding to condolences to express your gratitude. You choose one that best meets your needs.

AFFIRMATIONS:
- I am thankful for each day.
- I thankfully receive all the goodness that life brings my way.
- I am grateful for supportive friends and a loving family.

My Wish for YOU

May you find **PEACE** in your heart — remembering
it's more than a pump,
And feel compassion for **YOURSELF** and others.
May you experience **JOY** every day;
It gives you something to live for and gladdens the heart.
May you continue to share your **CARING** with others,
And let others **COMFORT** you when you are feeling down,
sad, or alone.
May you hang on during tough times — sometimes
that's all you can do;
But remember to let **HOPE** float up and do its magic healing.
May you remember to **BREATHE** when faced with fear, stress or loss;
It relaxes the body and refocuses the mind.
May you make time for **YOURSELF** each and every day
Practicing self-care and becoming your best.
May you recognize you are worthy and loved by **GOD** and others,
So you can share this **LOVE** with others too.
May you **LIVE** every day as if it were your last,
So you have no regrets.
May you have the courage to be **AWESOME**,
And hold tightly to the wonderful person you are.

Thank you from my HEART
Cheryl A. Barrett, 11/25/2014

Allow for Time
to Heal Your Wounded Spirit

*You don't know how strong you are until being strong
is the only option you have.*

— Bob Marley, Songwriter, Musician

Yes, it takes time to work through grief and loss.

There is no specified time limit for this journey. It is unique to each person. There is no one path for all, but a path exists for each of us to walk. These five actions helped me on my journey:

- *Be patient.* There will be ups and downs, progress and setbacks, on this healing journey.
- *Be strong.* Use your resources and reach out to family and friends to support you.
- *Have faith.* Move confidently toward the future filled with endless possibilities.
- *Look back.* Express joy and gratitude for what you shared.
- *Look forward.* Live with joy and gratitude in anticipation of your future.

While finishing this book, I reviewed the textbooks that I used in a Stress Management Instructor course I had taken some years ago. I found a section on stress and human spirituality, addressing the issues and impact of loss.

Some view this spiritual loss as a heart-sick feeling devastating to the soul. Yes, it does feel this way and goes on for some time. Your mind, your heart, and your soul are at war with the healing process at first. As time moves on, your mind shows you the logic of the situation, leading the way to healing as you set positive intentions. Your heart and soul continue to ache and recovery lags woefully behind, creating extended sorrow and grief.

The war within me went on for some time before I could take small steps toward healing. Yes, this war within is often said to be a trip to hell. **I agree!**

According to holistic stress management speaker B. L. Seaward, Ph.D: "There are two ways to emerge from a proverbial trip to hell. The first is as a victim, where one carries a sense of remorse or resentment for a very long time — sometimes forever. The second is as a victor, an individual who emerges gracefully with neither animosity nor resentment."

Dr. Seaward mentions that the journey of healing requires "exercising your muscles of the soul." Using his list of topics, I explain next how I exercised "the muscles of the soul" to heal my own wounded spirit from the loss of my dear husband, Fred.

- *Compassion*: I accepted comfort and compassion from friends and family who listened to me and shared in my grieving. I asked for help, hugs, or companionship when I felt the need. I read and reread the condolence cards and emails, finding comfort in the loving words. I am truly grateful for such caring sent my way. I also was compassionate toward myself, accepting my weaknesses. I allowed myself to cry. I even bravely chose events that brought on the tears, so I could purge myself of the pain of loss. Watching movies that involved loss and healing were very helpful, and I felt much better.

- *Courage:* I protected myself from triggers that would cause me to cry at times. I wore sunglasses to camouflage my eyes and hide the ravages of a tearful face. I carried tissues everywhere to mop up the waterfall of tears. I wanted people to see a survivor, not a victim of a tragedy…and someone with a brave heart who could stand tall and move forward. Writing this book took courage I did not think I had.

- *Creativity:* I found things that brought joy and laughter back into my life and put a smile on my face. I saw a "how to" video on making baskets out of recycled paper rolled into long tubes and made a few of these. The finished project was satisfying. In another creative adventure, three of us went to a "wine and paint night" at a local restaurant and painted a big sunflower with acrylics. We adopted artists' personas: I am now known as (Cherylbrant) and my accomplices were my friend, Peg (Pegasso), and my daughter, Bonnie (Boninchi): each imitating her favorite artist with her painting. We had fun.

- *Curiosity:* I sought out options and answers to so many questions about finances, funeral details, insurance, IRAs, 401Ks, death benefits, who needs death certificates, applying for social security, retirement, name change and beneficiary change. And so much more. I made lists upon lists and checked off items as they were done — eventually.

- *Faith:* I had faith from the start, although it was battered down by the nearly overwhelming grief, anger and regrets. Although my faith was wounded, I still watched the Sunday service with Joel Osteen. I still read my daily devotions on T*he Power of Being Thankful* by Joyce Meyer. I still prayed. I kept searching for understanding until I reread the story of Job in the *Bible*. Job experienced numerous losses and kept his faith. I found that you might never get the answers as to why this tragedy happened, but in faith, you walk forward, confident that there is a light waiting for you ahead.

- ***Forgiveness:*** This was hard, but I did forgive my husband for leaving me. I forgave God for taking him. I forgave myself for all the perceived regrets I had of not doing as much as I could have and should have done. I chose to give up the overpowering unforgiveness that kept eroding my spirit. It was such a relief.

- ***Humbleness:*** I worked to get outside of myself, helping others not as fortunate as I am. Looking at the big picture, my loss was insignificant compared to what some others have had to deal with in their life. I put together a care package for a friend, Anne, who always gives to others...so she would take time for herself, for a change. I mentored a young woman, June, in her pursuit of higher education in nursing. I gave my ticket to the amusement park to someone else to go. I volunteered to work on a quilt that was to be raffled off to raise money for the church. I cooked a meal and packed up a goodie bag for a friend whose husband underwent surgery. These actions helped me stop being focused on "poor me," and I am thankful for the opportunity to do these. I look forward to doing more in the future.

- ***Humor:*** I am blessed to live with a daughter who makes me laugh hard and often. We laugh about memories with my husband, her father. We laugh about almost anything. She often breaks into a song and dance that is hysterical. She still hides sometimes and tries to scare me like her father used to do to both of us. I watched movies alone that were funny, as well as watching ones with my daughter or with a friend and laughed a lot. My daughter was, and is, the greatest gift in keeping me smiling and stimulating laughter. I think she was a comedian in her past life. I knew that laughter heals, and I employed my creativity to make opportunities for it to happen. Laughter was a great tension reducer for me.

- ***Integrity:*** I fell short in "honesty" at first, as I needed to insulate myself from the pain and loss. Certainly, it was evident to many how devastating to me Fred's death was, but to others who were not close, things looked "OK." I told people I was fine when I was not, that I was eating when I was not, that I was sleeping when I was not — and more. As the impact of my grief lessened somewhat and time moved forward, I was able to find a way to trust others and share how I really felt. It was hard to keep up the "good lie" and such a relief to be able to share how I truly felt. I discovered that once I faced and became my truth again, I could become empowered and exercise other muscles of the soul more effectively.

- *Intuition:* Sensing, insights, inspiration, and enlightenment are part of intuition. I have had experience with intuition in the past. For example, my intuition told me that the first person (male) I met in Home Depot was the one to help me with my car issue in the parking lot, but I dismissed it. Fortunately, I had the opportunity to return to him, and he was the one who came and helped start my car. Often, we get a feeling about something and dismiss it, moving forward at a too-fast mental pace. Slowing down and taking a pause to reflect allows for opportunities to become more evident. I am thankful that when I was walking up the stairs the night my husband died, I acted on the feeling that I had and turned to look at him and say, "Good night, Fred" — the last time I spoke to him. I am now more sensitive to my intuition for self-care and for caring for others' needs.

- *Optimism:* Being positive was a challenge, as I had lost someone who was a constant source of support — my personal cheerleader of positivity. Suddenly, I had to create my own positivity. I found it is much easier to be negative and find fault than to be positive. So, I discovered a way to start. I faked being positive at first, and then little-by-little I began to feel positive about something in my day. I woke up and expressed thankfulness for the day. I set an intention to allow hope to bloom in my heart and open my eyes to a new future. I saw people struggling with much worse situations than mine, leading me to get out of my own way. I embraced a spirit of optimism.

- **Patience:** I grieved hard…with tears, anger, frustration, and more. I questioned God: *Why did you do this to me?* I questioned my dead husband: *Why did you do this to me?* I asked: *Why did I deserve to be alone?* I looked around at other older couples and envied them their togetherness and asked again: *Why not me?* Guess what? There were no answers, only acceptance that one time is over and another time is beginning. With patience and the passing of time, I came to terms with this. I felt peace.

- **Persistence:** To deal with all the details on my journey required persistence, because there were always loose ends. Nothing got done in a one-time action. There were always follow-ups, often too many to keep track of them all. I just made new lists and kept going.

- **Resiliency:** There were many times that I regressed in the healing process, but I did not give up. I bounced back stronger after every new wave of grief, anger, regret or self-pity that hit me, threatening to take me under. Each time, I chose to be strong and go forward; I bounced back quicker and was able to move forward again…and again…and again.

- **Unconditional love:** I worked for only four and a half months after my loss. I quit, to get out of the rat race and to be able to take better care of myself. I still mourned, even as I opened a new door to my future. I learned to love myself. The most amazing thing happened: I have become filled with more joy, peace, happiness, and expectation for sharing with others.

You can use the form at the end of this section with these same topics to write how you have exercised the muscles of your soul as you journey through your own grief and loss. It took time for me to do this, and it was sporadic, but thoughts and experiences along the way produced what I have shared about the muscles of the soul to me.

Yes, this journey is hard and it may be a long one. Be strong, and walk forward step-by-step, breath-by-breath. You, too, will emerge the victor. You have learned much and have much to share now with others.

AFFIRMATIONS:
- I step forward in faith and am stronger each day.
- I use the muscles of the soul to heal my wounded spirit.
- I am optimistic that I can experience joy and love.

Muscles of the Soul Worksheet

Take a few moments, when you are ready, to record how you exercised these muscles during a stressful event. You can also use this exercise in a proactive manner by brainstorming how you might develop or strengthen your muscles of the soul to provide a tool kit from which to draw when dealing with stress or to help others deal with stress. A good exercise for building resilience. (Continued on next page.)

- Compassion:

- Courage:

- Creativity:

- Curiosity:

- Faith:

- Forgiveness:

- Humbleness:

- Humor:

- Integrity:

- Intuition:

- Optimism:

- Patience:

- Persistence:

- Resiliency:

- Unconditional Love:

Witness to Others What You Have Learned on Your Journey

I don't know; I think I'd be gloomy without some faith that there is a purpose and there is a kind of witness to my life.

— John Updike, Novelist

These are words that I take to heart. I have often thought, *what good is it if I kept what I learned and experienced to myself while I watch others suffer?*

We all learn many valuable lessons on our journey through life. As children, we are taught many lessons about what to do and how to behave daily. We grow older and learn new lessons as we have different experiences, some good and some not so good. As parents, we try to share these lessons with our children, hoping they do not make the same mistakes we made. Aging occurs, and we learn even more lessons of life. Lessons that are valuable, but do we recognize the value of these lessons? Do we keep them to ourselves or do we offer them up to help others?

I have wanted to help others all my life, with what I knew and what I've learned so their lives would be easier, their suffering not as acute, hoping they'd skip some of the pain in the process. Yes, I was a compulsive helper in this respect; being a nurse helped to meet that need. But, I have learned that not everyone loves to hear, "Let me tell you what I learned, so you don't make the same mistakes."

Some, even most, people were not interested. They wanted to go their own ways, make their own mistakes and live their own lives. *OK, then,* I thought, *they have a right to run their own lives.* This hurt, but I have always been willing to learn, to try to do better…even if it took years. And it did.

But what if you could approach this sharing of life's lessons in another way? I thought. I learned that there are many ways to do this that are more effective and that maintain respect for others.

One way is to be a witness to others. A witness, according to the *Merriam-Webster Dictionary,* is "…one who has personal knowledge of something, something serving as evidence or proof, public affirmation by word or example…."

During my journey through my grief and loss, I learned a lot. Each day, even now, I am learning: how to go on alone, how to find purpose, how to find peace and joy, how to be brave, how to help others with what I learned…and to bear witness.

I have always wanted to write a book, but I never had a clear direction as to the content. The death of my husband was the stimulus for me to pursue this dream…although I did not recognize it at first. I was only journaling my thoughts, terrified that I would forget some part of what occurred. And then, something amazing happened. Interactions with people during this time stimulated words that became written down as stories and lessons learned.

Writing this book became my purpose and a learning opportunity for me about how to share and care for others. In this book, I tell my story, bearing witness to my journey: the sadness, grief, humor, progress and setbacks, helpful tips, and encouragement.

I hope you, too, can be a witness to others who are going through grief and loss. I urge you to provide caring, compassion, and support…instead of telling others how they should grieve or how long it should take.

Encourage with gentleness and love those who are suffering.

Be a Witness!

Resources

(Some resources focus on providing the survivor support services, while others focus on providing guidance or instructions on how healthcare professionals can support survivors of grief and loss.)

BOOKS: (Just a few. I suggest visiting your local book store or doing a Google search. I prefer looking in the store as I can better decide what book is best for me.)

Checklist for Family & Survivors, by Sally Balch Hurme (2 books: 2014 or 2015) Published by AARP.

This book provides many helpful suggestions in checklist format very useful for those going through the grieving process. I wish I would have known about this resource sooner.

Heart Humor Healing, by Patty Wooten, RN (1994). Published by Commune-a-key.

This book offers patients, their families, and health care providers an alternative perspective to the sometimes frightening and frustrating experience of hospitalization and the challenges of illness. It is a collection of quotes about heart, humor, and healing that will touch, tickle and titillate everyone.

Stressed is Desserts Spelled Backward: Rising above life's challenges with humor, hope and courage, by Brian Luke Seaward, PhD (2007). Published by Whole Person Associates.

This book contains stories of love and humor, shared by real people — their stories of stress, survival, and peace. A good read for anyone.

The Art of Calm: Relaxation Through the Five Senses, by Brian Luke Seaward, PhD (1999). Published by Health Communications, Inc.

This book takes you on a journey through the five senses and provides examples in each of how you can use everyday experiences of the senses to achieve relaxation.

When Things Fall Apart: Heart Advice for Difficult Times, by Perma Chodron (1997). Published by Random House, Inc.

This book provides heart advice for difficult times: ways to use painful emotions to cultivate wisdom, compassion and courage; methods for communicating that lead to openness and true intimacy with others; practices for reversing negative habitual patterns and techniques for working with chaotic situations. (A more spiritual view.)

WEBSITES: (There are numerous websites to consider. These are only a few.)

Dying in America at (www.dyinginamerica.org) is a multimedia documentary project, directed by award-winning filmmaker Carolyn Jones, that examines the dying experience through the eyes of nurses.

"It is our greatest hope that this website will offer some direction, comfort, and community for anyone facing these difficult times. Our Topics Page seeks to help you address specific issues you may be grappling with, or questions you may have. Our Tools Page seeks to help you discern, document and discuss your end of life wishes through a series of document-based steps."

"We will never defeat death, but we can prepare ourselves and our loved ones for what lies ahead and make the experience of dying as rich and as meaningful as the experience of living."

International Nurse Coach Association at (www.inurse.com) is an organization that provides training to nurses interested in becoming certified nurse coaches. These nurse coaches are trained to provide a person-centered, holistic, integrated body-mind-spirit perspective to healing along the continuum of life. Some have had special training in nutrition as well as end-of-life care. Nurses can visit this site to find out more about how to become a certified nurse coach. Anyone interested in contracting with a nurse coach can visit the site and go to "contact us" to request the names of nurse coaches in your area.

National Home Funeral Alliance at (homefuneralalliance.org) — The NHFA empowers families to care for their own dead by providing educational opportunities and connections to resources that promote environmentally sound and culturally nurturing death practices. This is the place to find information about home funerals, including directories for where to find home funeral guides, home funeral education programs, home-funeral-friendly funeral directors, celebrants and clergy, and groups who will help families when needed.

Sacred Crossings at (sacredcrossings.com) — Their mission is to educate and support individuals toward a conscious, peaceful transition and to empower and guide families to reclaim the healing ritual of a home funeral. To explore this option, review their FAQs.

Huntington Meditation and Imagery Center at (huntingtonmeditation.com) — is an organization dedicated to bringing transpersonal understanding and transpersonal skills into the health and helping professions. By knowing how to awaken these qualities in your patients, clients, students, employees, congregants and others who come to you for help, you bring an added healing dimension to your work. Visit their website for details and class options for health care professionals, social workers, clergy and others. I used a lot of their techniques to assist me in my grief work.

Grief Share at (griefshare.org) — There are many websites to provide support for various grief and loss categories: loss of a spouse, partner, child, pet. They may even be called GriefShare groups. These may be located in a hospital, a church or residential home. Many sites to look through to find one that fits your needs.

Facebook — If you search "grief support groups" on Facebook, you will find a list of options to explore. This venue provides a broader access for connecting to others experiencing grief. This is quite public with interactions from unknown sources. Some may choose this, while others prefer a more personal support group.

Bereavement Support Group — Another term to google for options of grief support online.

Hospice Foundation at (hospicefoundation.org).Then go to section on **End-of-Life-Support-and-Resources/Grief-Support/Support-Groups** — They provide some education about grief and loss. There is also a list of Support Group Resources:

The Compassionate Friends — Support after the death of a child.

AARP Grief and Lost Resource — Support after the death of a senior.

National Widower's Organization — Support for men grieving a loss.

American foundation for Suicide Prevention — Support for suicide survivors.

Griefnet — An organization of support for adults grieving a loss.

Hellogrief — An organization of support for adults and kids grieving a loss.

OTHER: (Community resources)

Physician referrals to certified counselors: Your physician can offer you support, as well as direct you to qualified counselors certified in supporting emotional and psychological issues during grief and loss.

Friends and family: Consider this option as a strategy for real-time 24/7 support as your base of support, if it is available to you. Make a list of those who would be good resources in your time of need so it is readily available.

Local Churches

Hospital Support Groups

About the Author

Cheryl A. Barrett, MSN, RN, NC-BC, has been a nurse for over 30 years and is a board-certified nurse coach by the American Holistic Nurses Association Credentialing Center. As a nurse, she was always drawn to the psychosocial needs of patients recognizing that the patient was much more than their illness.

She believes that stress can have a significant impact on the mind/body/spirit resulting in distress of the "whole person." No one is exempt from stress! However, stress can be modified, controlled, and in some cases — eliminated. Through her training as a Holistic Stress Management Instructor, Cheryl gained invaluable skills to support herself and others to decrease stress and achieve work-life balance. She promotes self-care as an essential component of any stress management program and has used many of the stress management techniques during her own life challenges, most recently coping with the death of her spouse. She has also been a speaker on this topic to local senior citizen groups.

In her role as a nurse coach, she has mentored students pursuing their bachelor's and master's degree in nursing to successful completion. She helped them feel more confident; improve decision-making, communication and leadership skills; and increase their personal effectiveness in accomplishing personal goals. Both academic learning expertise and guidance for achieving work-life balance were provided and supported self-care as an integral component of practice.

Writing has always been an interest of Cheryl's. She has created newsletters, poems, and published articles in issues of Phi Kappa Phi's *Forum* and the American Holistic Nurses Association's *Beginnings*.

Currently, she is an active member of the Mooresville Art Gallery in Mooresville, NC, and supports the town's soup kitchen with profits from her paper crafts.

Cheryl resides in North Carolina with her daughter, Bonnie.

For more information, contact her at:

Gmail — c.a.barrett116@gmail.com
Linkedin.com — Cheryl Ann Barrett, RN, MSN, NC-BC
Outskirts Press Author Webpage — www.outskirtspress.com/
goodgrief
FaceBook — fb.me/GoodGrief.CherylABarrett

Review This Book

Please consider reviewing *Good Grief.* Reviewers help writers and their audience find each other.

Cheryl A. Barrett and her potential readers would benefit from having you review this book on, for example: amazon.com or at OutSkirts Press Author Page — outskirtspress.com/goodgrief.

Please visit Cheryl's FaceBook page to provide a review, ask questions, make comments, share posts with others and take advantage of helpful content related to grief and loss. **FaceBook** — fb.me/GoodGrief. CherylABarrett.